Creating Smart Schools

Creating Smart Schools

The Education Instructional Coaching Model

Dr. Judith Kronin

Library of Congress Control Number:		2011910354
ISBN:	Hardcover	978-1-4628-9165-8
	Softcover	978-1-4628-9166-5
	Ebook	978-1-4628-9167-2

This book was printed in the United States of America.

To order additional copies of this book, contact:
Xlibris Corporation
1-888-795-4274
www.Xlibris.com
Orders@Xlibris.com
99358

CONTENTS

ACKNOWLEDGEMENTS

I extend my sincere gratitude to the many dedicated teachers, administrators, school district personnel, and parents that I have worked with over the past forty years. You inspired me to always keep children first and to stand firm on the commitment that affords all students a quality education. There is a special place in my heart for the Orange Middle School Instructional Team. A special thanks is given to the small learning coordinators and members of the building team: Dr. Howell, Ms. Sica, Ms. Phibs, Mrs. Nails, Ms. Mondestin, Mrs. Rembert, Mrs. Harper, Dr. Young, Mr. Medley, Mr. Smith, Mrs. Sacks, Ms. Wynn, and Mrs. Berry. Your professional efforts, enduring spirits and powerful drives transformed our school into a learning center that has repeatedly proved to be the standard for other schools to follow.

Dr. Terry Russo, thank you for your generous support and encouragement. Your extensive knowledge of instruction is greatly appreciated. Dr. Erma Malloy, thank you for the years of encouragement. Cheryl Harden, thank you for lending your skills and expertise to this project. Deborah Carroll, thank you for sharing your knowledge from a master teacher's perspective. Dr. Penelope Lattimer, thank you for being my mentor and guiding force.

My sisters and brother, Barbara Wise, Carol Bradley, and Marion Bates Jr., are acknowledged for their understanding and support of this book as an important part of our history. To my children, Shawn Sampson, Amanda Gregurich, Esq., Dr. Shayna Jones, and Karen Campis, Esq., thank you for always offering me words of encouragement. To my nephew, Louren Bates, thank you for all of your astute advice and technical expertise. To my grandchildren, Denett Rivera, Shannon Sampson, Shawn Sampson, JD Campisi, Jake Campisi, Anna Gregurich, Katie Campisi, Caleb Jones, James Gregurich, and Aiden Jones, this is my gift to you and my greatest joy is for you to use *Creating Smart Schools* to guide others.

My appreciation is extended to Anna Go and all members of Xlibris for their assistance and support.

To my husband Ed, the love of my life, thank you for your support, kindness, and expertise. Your rich conversations reaffirmed the importance of writing this book. Thank you for sharing your brilliant mind.

Lastly, I thank all educators, our unsung heroes for taking the most important profession in our society very seriously.

Dr. Judith Kronin

FOREWORD

Public education has been under fire and continues to be the target of dissatisfaction. The 1983 "A Nation at Risk: The Imperative for Education Reform Report," by President Ronald Reagan's Commission on Excellence in Education, is still considered a landmark event in public education. "We report to the American people that while we can take justifiable pride in what our schools and colleges have historically accomplished and contributed to the United States and the well-being of its people, the educational foundations of our society are presently being eroded by a rising tide of mediocrity that threatens our very future as a Nation and a people. What was unimaginable a generation ago has begun to occur—others are matching and surpassing our educational attainments." Among the findings from studies that were surveyed was a report which indicated that the average SAT score dropped over 50 points in the verbal section and nearly 40 points in the mathematics section over a seventeen year period from 1963-1980. The recommendations were to strengthen local and state requirements for graduation and to adopt more rigorous standards. With little hesitation, American public schools quickly responded to this admonishment.

The Standards Movement followed. As of 2001 forty-nine states and the District of Columbia have academic standards. This reform was designed to address the concerns raised by the "A Nation at Risk" report." It resulted in the federal Elementary and Secondary Education Act (ESEA) 2000, the forerunner to No Child Left Behind (NCLB). These standards included: Academic Standards, referring to what students should know and be able to do in core academic subjects at each grade level; Content Standards, referring to a basic agreement about the body of education knowledge that all students should know; and Performance Standards, referring to the level of performance which is good enough to be described as advanced, proficient or below basic.

Diane Ravitch, a research professor of education at New York University as well as a historian of education and Assistant Secretary of education in the administration of President George H. W. Bush, led the creation of state and national standards. In her most recent book, The Death and Life of the Great American School System: How

Testing and Choice Are Undermining Education (2010), she states that she used the word death in her title "to warn that our nation is at a perilous moment and public education is in danger." Further, she states, "having supported these policies in the past, I felt a need to explain why I now reject them and see they won't help to improve education but actually harm it and set our nation and children back." Writing in the Wall Street Journal on March 9, 2010, Ravitch states "High stakes testing, 'utopian goals' draconian penalties, school closings, privatization, and charter schools didn't work." She concluded that the best predictor of low academic performance is "poverty–not bad teachers."

The present author is not only aware of the pressures and challenges that confront public education, she is also cognizant of the day to day balancing act that educators face deciding between what they desire for their students and what they must do because of the many stringent mandates. However, she stills holds fast to the words of Horace Mann, "the father of American education," "The common school is the greatest discovery ever made."

While the author does not believe in the cliché of one size fits all, she is a strong proponent that it will be educators and not politicians nor entrepreneurs that will offer the solutions to the problems facing our nation's school system. *Creating Smart Schools* is a book designed for teachers and administrators who recognize that any school or district can become effective if they employ the Education Instructional Coaching Model (EICM) which requires a curriculum that includes quarterly benchmarks and assessments; an infrastructure that accommodates a community of learners, an instructional staff that employs effective an instructional strategies, and an instructional coaching model. The model sets the bar high to ensure that all students are provided maximum opportunities to engage in educational settings that inspire critical thinking, and a joy of learning.

Orange, New Jersey is the setting for this unique book on school reform.

DEDICATION

This book, *Creating Smart Schools,* is dedicated to my parents Lillie Mae and Marion Bates Sr. and my brother, Leonard Bates who passed away on April 16, 2011. Mom and Dad, thank you for being superb educational role models. Your life lessons have endured the test of time. Leonard, thank you for the inspiration that you left to me, and to all members of our family.

Lovingly,

Judy

Education is not a preparation for life, education is life itself.

—John Dewey

CREATING SMART SCHOOLS

Summary

I am a veteran educator committed to public education. I believe that we can provide quality instruction to all students attending public and private schools. Ron Edmonds spoke in an uncompromising voice, "All children can learn." Today I speak with the same resounding spirit and say, "All educators can teach." America takes national test scores very seriously. The Education Instructional Coaching Model (EICM), which I propose, will once again enable American students to earn top scores on the Programme for International Students Assessment (PISA). EICM evolved from research and a set of core beliefs, which include the following:

- The major goal of educators is to inspire students to become critical thinkers and independent learners.
- Educators must create environments of small learning communities where a major portion of instruction is devoted to problem solving.
- Educators must create lesson plans that inspire students to increase their enjoyment of good questions and help them work out their own understanding of "static" knowledge like mathematics, science, and reading.
- Teachers must design student-directed instructions.
- Educational reform is comprehensive and involves every member of the educational community.

- Instructional coaching, which requires mutual respect between a coach and teacher, is the cornerstone for improving classroom instruction.

This book offers a process for the creation of smart or *effective* schools through the development and implementation of the Education Instructional Coaching Model. This model makes it possible for every student to attain a quality education.

The foundation of every state is the education of its youth.

—Diogenes Laertius

Background of Orange Public School District and the City of Orange Township

Orange Public School District is located in northern New Jersey, approximately twenty-five miles from New York. At the time, the district included a preschool, a high school, an alternative high school, eight elementary schools, a middle school, with a total enrollment of approximately 5,300 students. The Orange Public School District has a long legacy of living up to its motto of "keeping children first."

The origin of the city of Orange can be traced back to 1666 to a New Haven, Connecticut, colony. Orange was officially incorporated as a city in 1860; in 1872, it was reincorporated, and in 1982, the name was changed to the city of Orange Township.

Hat making was the essential industry, and it flourished until 1892. Prominent hatters, including Stetson, shoemakers, and brewers created an industrial city that employed a significant number of immigrants. By 1892, the twenty-one hat-making firms employed 3,700 people in plants and were valued at 1.1 million dollars. Millions of hats left Orange, New Jersey, bound for the four corners of the globe. By 1921, only five firms were left; and by 1960, all were closed. Like hat making, brewing beer was a big industry in Orange. Liebmann Breweries Inc. was one of the largest breweries and bottled for Rheingold Beer. This industry closed its doors in 1977.

Baseball player Monte Irvin, heavyweight boxer Tony Galento, first African American member of New Jersey legislation Walter G. Alexander, Beatrice Alice Hick, the founder of the Society of Women Engineers, actor Roy Schneider, defense tackle for the New York Giants Jay Alford, and basketball player for NBA's New York Knicks Al Harrington are among the notable citizens born and raised in Orange, New Jersey.

The city of Orange Township remains a port-of-entry city. As of 2008, of the approximately 5,300 students enrolled in the Orange public schools, 12 percent spoke Creole or French at home; 14 percent spoke Spanish. Other languages that are spoken at home are Dutch, Portuguese, Yoruba, Ibo, Mandingo, Amharic, Ashanti, Akan, and Twi. While 75 percent of the city was identified as African American in the 2000 census, the school population has shown an increase in Hispanic students. Approximately 79 percent of the students receive free or reduced lunch, and this same source of data reported 15.4 percent of the families of Orange lived below the poverty level.

The greatest good that you can do for another is not to share your riches, but to reveal to him his own.

—Benjamin Disraeli

INTRODUCTION

On Monday, the fourth of January 2010, I invited my sister Barbara to join me for a visit to my daughter's home in West Orange, New Jersey. She agreed, and the date was set for Friday, January 8. My thoughts were that this is going to be interesting for both of us since this was the first time that she was meeting her great four-month-old nephew, and of course, I love spending time with my grandson and my daughter. With snow in the forecast for Friday, we left Thursday. It's a forty-five-mile trip from Westbury, New York, to West Orange, New Jersey, and involves crossing New York City's Throgs Neck and George Washington Bridges and the very unpredictable Cross Bronx Expressway. During the trip, my sister asked if it was possible to visit Park Avenue Elementary School in Orange, the elementary school that she attended as a child. This was fine since Park Avenue Elementary School is located only a few miles from my daughter's house; and as a former interim superintendent of Orange Public School District, I looked forward to revisiting the staff and the principal I had worked with.

We arrived Thursday evening and were shocked by my grandson's impressive size and his newly developed personality. I immediately noticed he was a little burst of energy. All he wanted to do was play. He pleaded to be placed in a variety of physical positions from which he could bounce, jump, and display his captivating smile. He was happy to show us all his favorite moves. Caleb's physical activities were hilarious to watch, and we enjoyed each of them. In a matter of minutes, we learned all his favorite moves; and the bonus was, it was great exercise, for improving our upper-body strength. We lifted him above our heads and below our knees until bedtime, and the next morning, we began the routine for his care. His schedule was not for the faint of heart; he quickly let us know that he was in charge. It was not long before he had his aunt, his mom, and I scampering around, meeting all his demands. We responded to every sound and body movement like robots, and we loved every minute of it.

On Friday morning, as my daughter, Shayna, who is a doctor specializing in obstetrics and gynecology, was preparing for work, I informed her that my sister and I wanted to visit Park Avenue Elementary School. Fortunately, she was able to arrange her schedule to accommodate our plans. I placed a call to the principal of Park Avenue Elementary School to inform him that we wanted to take a tour of his school. His secretary informed me that he was in a meeting and asked me if she should interrupt the meeting for the call. I asked her to have the principal return my call after his scheduled meeting, and the visitation was arranged. My daughter accompanied us on this visit.

Chapter One

When you do the common things in life in an uncommon way,
you will command the attention of the world.

—George Washington Carver

Park Avenue Elementary School

As Shayna parked her car near the entrance to Park Avenue Elementary School, she and Barbara expressed how impressed they were with the reconstruction of the school. As we entered the building, my mind quickly focused on my family's personal history in the Orange school system, recent events that related to the reconstruction of Park Avenue Elementary School, and my professional experience in Orange Public School District.

For reasons that I can't articulate, I had not taken time to reflect upon the importance of this visit. However, my mood quickly changed when Elsie, a Park Avenue Elementary School security guard, gave me a hug and said, "We miss you." I reciprocated my feelings to her. I asked her how things were going at their beautifully reconstructed school. She responded by saying, "Things are going so well" and that teachers take pleasure in knowing that they don't have to remind students to keep their school clean. Elsie mentioned that her only complaint was that there was a blind spot, which prevented her from having a full view of the entrance of the building. However, judging from her mannerisms, a solution was in hand. As I listened to her raspy voice, I realized how much I missed the interactions with her and the staff of Park Avenue Elementary School.

As Elsie spoke, my cell phone rang; it was Dr. Hackett, the principal, returning my morning call. I informed him that I was in his building for a tour of his impressive school, and shortly thereafter, he came down and took my family and me on a tour of his school, which made me teary eyed. Interestingly enough, it was only when I saw

Dr. Hackett that I began experiencing a feeling that my family had come full circle. The irony of being born a poor kid in this city, returning and becoming the interim superintendent seemed preposterous.

While my daughter and sister rattled off one superlative after another about the school's renovations and innovations, I was trying to grasp what this moment meant to our entire family. My parents had migrated from Aiken, South Carolina, to Orange, New Jersey, in 1941. At one point in our family history, my mother was the housekeeper for Mrs. Hoff, the principal of Park Avenue Elementary School. My mother and Mrs. Hoff had a close relationship, one that would impact every member of my family. Barbara, my older sister, who had suggested this visit, had attended Park Avenue Elementary School from 1944-1950. Similarly, two older brothers, Marion and Leonard, had also attended Park Avenue Elementary School. Leonard's, my oldest brother's story became the inspiration for all of the younger siblings to attain a good education. The story that was told to me was that Leonard was bullied at school and, therefore, did not like school and, consequently, frequently played hooky. As my siblings and I were growing up, my mother would often share stories with us about how in the early fifties, Leonard would be found shining shoes in the pool halls of Orange. She made it clear that without the support and encouragement that she received from Mrs. Hoff, the principal of Park Avenue Elementary School, he would not have graduated from Orange High School in 1955.

Before the family's move to Hempstead, New York, in 1955, Carol, a sister who is seventeen months my senior, and I attended Oakwood Avenue, another elementary school in Orange, New Jersey, from 1951 to 1955. My memories of the experience are vague and limited.

For a brief moment, as I was standing in the lobby of Park Avenue Elementary School, I reflected upon my rich and colorful past. I just stood there, contemplating the unlikelihood of me standing in the newly reconstructed and refurbished Park Avenue Elementary School, with my sister in awe of the transformation of her old school and me in awe that I had been the interim superintendent of schools in Orange. Meanwhile, as this was transpiring, I was sharing this moment with my daughter and my grandson.

After completing a thirty-five-year career in education in New York, I resumed a career in education in Orange, New Jersey; and after three challenging and effective years as an instructional leader at Orange Middle School, I became the interim superintendent of Orange public schools. Standing with my sister, my daughter, and my grandson reminded me of the significance of the moment; and if that was not enough excitement, I "felt" the presence of my deceased parents and the "joy" that they would have experienced by the knowledge of my being the educational leader of the Orange public schools.

My mind raced back to the September 10, 2009, ribbon-cutting ceremony for the official opening of the newly reconstructed Park Avenue Elementary School. Dignitaries including then–Governor Jon Corzine; Willa Spicer, assistant commissioner of education for the state of New Jersey; Kris Kolluri, the CEO of the New Jersey Schools Development Authority; Dr. Lawrence Feinsod, the Essex County executive superintendent of schools; Patricia Arthur, president of Orange Board of Education; Mila Jasey, the assembly woman of the 27th Legislative District, along with Mr. Ronald Lee, the newly appointed superintendent of Orange public schools; and Dr. Myron Hackett, the principal of Park Avenue School, his staff, and students were all present. This impressive body of dignitaries offered greetings and expounded upon their thoughts and vision for this incredible school. However, the moment belonged to the Park Avenue Elementary students who spoke from their hearts. They read poems and sang songs that they had created for this auspicious occasion in their young lives. As I sat there, I focused on the pomp and circumstances that were taking place.

The January 4 visit was very different. Unlike the previous event, I was not distracted by the dignitaries. Although on the previous occasion, I knew that my name was on the Park Avenue Elementary School dedication plaque, I failed to take a moment and observe it. It was not until later that day when I reflected upon the events of the celebration, I realized my failure.

As we waited for Dr. Hackett to take us on the tour, I asked Elsie about the location of the plaque, and she said, "It's right behind you, and your name is on it." I slowly turned around and made my way to the glass cabinet that housed this plaque, and there it was, my name, among others, who were instrumental in making the reconstruction of Park Avenue Elementary School possible. We all have defining moments in our lives, and this was one of those moments for me.

Park Avenue Elementary School was designed to be a green building with state-of-the-art amenities. The floor plan reflected the many planning meetings that my team and I attended in Trenton, New Jersey, where we had pushed for a facility that would not only look fantastic but would be designed to provide quality instruction for the students attending this school. Park Avenue Elementary School is not the first elementary K–8 building with two computer labs, two science labs, a dance studio, music rooms, media center, and a cafetorium. However, it is the first school that I have ever been in where I felt the design of the building inspired students to engage in critical thinking and independent learning. As we toured the three floors of the newly reconstructed Park Avenue Elementary School, my sister and daughter were shocked by the quality of instruction that they witnessed as they strolled from corridor to corridor, covering the three floors of the building. They repeatedly stated that they had never seen a school that operated as effectively as Park Avenue Elementary School. They were touched by the competitive nature of the students. They could clearly see from the responses of the students that the students not only understood the instruction that was being taught, but owned it. As we walked by classrooms, we saw students shaking their hands wildly to respond to the Socratic questions that were being posed; and in other instances, we saw students pondering in deep thought before they spoke. These were snapshots of "good instruction" at Park Elementary

School, I witnessed the fruits of the labor of an entire district that I was proud to be part of.

I realized that I was watching the Education Instructional Coaching Model (EICM) in action. In some classrooms, I observed accountable talk. In other classrooms, the students were clustered around their teacher and a smart board in a dialogue that included a wealth of Socratic questions and responses. I saw several classrooms where cooperative learning groups were in progress. The staff and students at Park Avenue Elementary School appeared to be fully engaged in teaching and learning. I took time to reflect upon the journey and the process that was involved, which led to the creation of the Education Instructional Coaching Model (EICM).

It is not fair to ask of others what you are not willing to do yourself.

—Eleanor Roosevelt

Main Street School

My brief experience as interim principal at Main Street School was a breakthrough moment in my career. It began with a phone call from a friend, Constance Frazier, the assistant superintendent for curriculum and instruction in Orange Public School District. She asked if I was interested in providing coverage for the principal of Main Street School, who was on medical leave. Although I was recently retired as principal of A. B. Davis Middle School in Mount Vernon, New York, my immediate response was yes. I had already begun to yearn to return to a school setting.

As I walked through Main Street School, my mind flashed back to my memories of my elementary school days at Oakwood Avenue School, a typical three-story brick facade, built during the mid-19th Century. Unlike Main Street School, which was a grades K–8 state-of-the-art facility, Oakwood Avenue School is one of several historical landmarks in the city of Orange Township.

The experience of returning to Orange as an interim principal is what I refer to as one of my "bucket items." Although it was not a conscious decision, I certainly treasured the prospect of being able to return to my childhood school district. When I entered Main Street School, I was pleasantly surprised by the staff's warm reception. Many of these staff members were bright young professionals who were transitioning into teaching from careers in law and finance. Their novice experience spawned the many classroom visitations that followed. Consequently, some of my most enjoyable times in my career were spent in classrooms of these new teachers as their instructional coach.

The administrative team was loosely organized and included an assistant principal and some members from the Child Study Team and reading and math coaches. With relatively little coaxing, we solidified into an instructional team. The administrative team and I witnessed teachers struggling with their subjects. After examining their lesson plans and patiently observing their teaching practices, we realized that the quality of their instruction could greatly improve if they employed better questioning techniques. We also realized that this was true for many of the veteran teachers as well. We recognized that many of the teachers had neither carefully thought about the questions that they posed to their students, nor thought about the impact that these questions had upon learning. We encouraged teachers to set the stage for whole-group instruction and to discuss how the instruction would personally improve their lives. Correct answers were not positively reinforced. We began a dialogue with the instructional staff about the use of the Socratic method and techniques for generating Socratic questions.

The important thing is not to stop questioning.

—Albert Einstein

Socratic Questioning

Administrators have limited time and opportunity for professional development; with that in mind, the administrative team at Main Street School initiated a plan to impact classroom instruction. Our classroom visits reflected a need for teachers to improve their questioning technique. The plan was simple: we would acquaint the instructional staff with Socratic questioning by engaging them in a demonstration of the Socratic method.

The Socratic questioning technique that was employed was based upon the definition of Socratic teaching, which focuses on giving students questions, not answers. One continuously probes the subject with questions. As the Socratic questioner, I acted as the logical voice, a voice that the mind develops when developing critical thinking skills. The plan was to deal fairly with each response from the faculty. All responses were followed up with further questions, and selected questions were posed to advance the discussion. This forced the faculty to respond in a disciplined, intelligent manner. As the Socratic questioner, I kept the discussion focused, kept the discussion intellectually responsible, stimulated the discussion with probing questions, and elicited questions from as many faculty members as possible.

Shortly into the faculty meeting, I began to employ the Socratic method. The instructional activity lasted ten to fifteen minutes. Basically, every question that was asked of me was answered with a question. It did not take the staff long to realize the benefit of this technique. They questioned their colleagues as well as themselves. They became more cognizant of the impact of the overall conversation. The discussion that followed indicated that the instructional staff was interested in a tool that would inspire their students to engage in critical thinking. To enable the staff to become more familiar with the use of the Socratic method, this experience was followed up with a Saturday workshop.

I was inspired by the level of interest emanating from the Main Street School staff, and the workshop reinforced the importance of embedded professional learning. Our limited time was used wisely. The instructional staff in Orange made it a practice to use the classrooms as their laboratories to custom design instructional strategies and practices.

I cannot teach anybody anything. I can make them think.

—Socrates

The Main Street School
Socratic Method Workshop

The staff sat in a Socratic circle, and using Socrates as the role model, I assumed my most befuddled expression and asked a series of questions, designed to inspire the staff to ignite their critical thinking skills and to become familiar with the six types of Socratic questions and their application.

To create the appropriate mind-set, I did not mix or mingle with any of the staff members prior to the beginning of this workshop.

Opening question—"For the life of me, I can't figure out where I am. Can anyone help me out? Where am I?" A teacher responded, "Dr. Kronin, you are at Main Street School in Orange, NJ."

Second question—"That's interesting!" I then asked someone else, "Do you agree with . . . ?" The teacher stated that he agreed.

Third question—"I don't mean to put anyone on the spot, but I am not convinced that I am at Main Street School, nor am I sure that this town is Orange, NJ. Can anyone provide me with evidence that would prove that I am at Main School and that this is the city of Orange?" The reaction was one of annoyance, but most of the teachers began to look through their personal materials for Main Street School stationery. A teacher handed me a copy of the faculty meeting attendance sheet, and it contained the name of the school, but it did not include the address.

Fourth question—"I don't know where this problem that I am having is going. Therefore, I must ask the question, will this evidence that you just presented hold up in a court of law?" That's when someone realized that their evidence failed to make a case for my location. Someone made a call and verified the address and location and someone else stated that they witnessed this and were willing to state this information under oath.

Fifth question—"Now that you have helped me establish my location, does anyone know why I am here?"

"You are here to facilitate a workshop on Socratic questioning."

Sixth question—"Could you repeat that? Did you say Socratic questioning or Socratic method?"

"I said Socratic questioning."

"What is the difference? Is one approach superior to the other? If so, why?"

Someone responded, "I am not sure. Socratic method is the process, and Socratic questioning is the technique that you employ when creating Socratic questions."

Seventh question—"What is Socratic questioning?"

"It's when someone asks questions that require the person to engage in critical thinking."

Eighth question—"Should any of this information be written down?"

Ninth question—"Is there any particular reason why this method is called the Socratic method?" A teacher said that it is named after the famous Greek philosopher Socrates, who taught his students by asking questions.

Tenth question—"What is the significance of asking Socratic questions?" A teacher said that it makes you think.

Eleventh question—"Can someone explain what critical thinking is?" A teacher responded that it causes us to take an in-depth look at our beliefs and the beliefs of others. I responded by asking, "Are you saying that it causes us to examine our belief system and the belief system of others?" Another teacher who was very excited to share her response said that it also makes us examine our assumptions and the assumptions of others. I responded by asking, "Are you saying it is a process that we use to reflect upon our assumptions and the assumptions of others?" Another teacher commented that it makes us think about our judgments and the judgments of others. I responded by asking, "Are you saying it's the mind-set that we use to make judgments that relate to ourselves and others?" A math teacher said that it is also related to deductive reasoning. He continued by saying that it is part of the system that we use when we make decisions by deductive reasoning. I responded by asking, "Are you saying that this is the process that we use to reach decisions through the deductive reasoning process?"

At this point, I shifted the workshop to a discussion that enabled the staff to gain insight into the six types of Socratic questions.

Twelfth question—For the conceptual clarification question—I referred back to the teacher who stated that the "Socratic method is a process and that Socratic questioning is the technique that is used when creating Socratic questions." I asked, "What exactly does that mean? How does that relate to what others have said? What did you already know about the difference between the two concepts before today's workshop?"

Thirteenth question—For probing assumptions, I asked, "What else can you assume about the Socratic method?" I asked, "What assumptions can you make about the Socratic method?" A teacher stated that one can assume that there is a relationship between the use of Socratic method and critical thinking. I asked, "Can someone follow up or expand upon this discussion?"

Fourteenth question—For probing rationale, reasons and evidence questions, I asked, "Can anyone verify or disprove that Socrates actually created the Socratic method?" A teacher stated that we can assume that he did since the method is named after him. I asked, "Is that proof?" Another teacher stated that it was not proof and she knew that it was his students that passed his teachings along and not Socrates himself. I asked her how she knew this. Someone else responded that Plato, who was also a Greek philosopher and a student of Socrates, who interpreted Socrates's teachings. I asked someone else if the reasoning for their responses were good enough. I asked them what authority they were basing this information on. Someone suggested a review of Plato's dialogues could provide us with a definitive answer.

Fifteenth question—For questioning viewpoints and perspectives, I asked the following questions: "Who benefits from using the Socratic method? What is the difference between the Socratic method and Socratic questioning? Why is it better to ask Socratic questions as opposed to objective questions? What is the difference?"

Sixteenth question—For questions that probe implications and consequences, I asked the following questions: "How can this instructional strategy be used in your classroom? How can this tool be used when you are developing your lesson plans? What implications can be anticipated? How will this technique impact your instruction? What impact did this instructional activity have upon your critical thinking skills?"

Seventeenth question—For questions about questions, I asked, "What was the point of me asking you the last question, which was 'What impact did this instructional activity have upon your critical thinking skills?'" My follow-up question was "Why did I ask that question? Does this discussion have meaning for you?"

Shortly after this workshop, teachers became more conscious of their use of Socratic questions. The assistant principal and I made a point of writing positive notes on the teachers' lesson plans when we saw evidence that they included the Socratic method and Socratic questions. When we visited grade-level meetings, we listened for evidence that this instructional strategy was included in their discussions.

This instructional initiative was important because it heightened the professionalism in the building. The administrative team began to hear comments about the application of the Socratic method. Later, when I reflected back on my experience at Main Street School, I realized how significant it is for an instructional staff to develop common language. The technique of identifying an instructional deficiency and developing an instructional strategy to address the deficiency became the cornerstone of our approach throughout my tenure in the Orange Public School District. Our administrative team had limited faith in professional development that was not embedded in classroom instruction. This also marked the first step for the instructional team at Main Street becoming a community of learners.

It is professionally challenging to develop a high-performing team. Just as the instructional staff expected their students to become astute learners, we expected the staff to become a community of learners. A community of learners doesn't just happen; they are intentionally created at every level of a school and organization (Lenz, 2007). Although I knew my time as interim principal of Main Street School was limited, it was important to maintain high expectations during my ten weeks of coverage.

Another indication of the team's appreciation of their newly acquired instructional resource came on the heels of the first workshop. Ms. Frazier, assistant superintendent for curriculum and instruction, directed our staff to develop strategies to improve eighth-grade English Language Arts state assessment scores. The staff planned a Saturday workshop utilizing the Socratic method to analyze the data and develop an instructional initiative to address areas of assessment where the students did not attain the expected proficient and advanced-proficient scores. The usual negative approach was replaced by positive optimism, and this positive attitude was apparent during the workshop. The school facilitator led a discussion, which was a series of Socratic questions that were based upon the data from the eighth-grade scores of the ELA Assessment. These Socratic questions were designed to enable the teachers of this workshop to write prescriptive questions or measurable goals. After writing several measurable goals, the team took a break, and I asked participating teachers why they were so confident; they said, "We have an instructional tool that enables us to complete the assignment."

The implementation of Socratic questioning at Main Street was not without setbacks. The resistance reminded the administrative team of the difficulty associated with organizational change. Some teachers included a series of Socratic questions in their lesson plans, yet when we visited their classrooms, there was no evidence these teachers were asking the questions in the classroom. In some instances, the teachers reverted to the distribution of worksheets. Upon seeing this ineffective practice, we refused to rush to judgment. Instead, conferences were scheduled with these teachers after each informal observation. The administrative team and the teachers collaboratively developed plans to rectify the problem. We began our discussion by referring to Bloom's taxonomy. After a discussion of their instructional lesson in terms of the categories of Bloom's taxonomy—knowledge, comprehension, application, analysis, synthesis, and evaluation—we discussed their instructional lesson in terms of preplanned questions and emerging questions. The teachers reviewed and interpreted the meaning of preplanned questions as meaning new concepts, questions that steered the discussion in a certain direction, and questions designed to focus the discussion on certain items to identify student knowledge on the topic. The emerging questions were interpreted as those questions that evolved as a result of specific responses to the preplanned questions. Engaging the teachers in discussions, which involved a more in-depth understanding of effective questioning, enabled the teachers to gain a greater insight into the application and practice of the sixth type of Socratic question. Later, the administrative team at Main Street and other schools within Orange would refer to this process as making an instructional strategy "user-friendly." My experience at Main Street School taught me that teachers appreciate classroom support. In the past, too much instructional time was spent looking for instructional flaws and making minimal effort to improve and support effective classroom practices.

The important lessons that we learned from the Main Street staff were, when there is an instructional deficiency, (1) develop an instructional strategy and an accompanying workshop that can successfully address that instructional deficiency, (2) monitor improvement via evidence in teachers' lesson plans and implementation of the practice(s) in teachers' classrooms, and (3) always give teachers credit for academic accomplishments that are achieved in a school. This became a practice that administrative team would follow throughout my tenure in Orange.

As simple as it sounds, this can have a profound impact upon improving instruction and ultimately increasing academic achievement. Needless to say, it was bittersweet when the principal returned ten weeks later. I was pleased that my efforts led to a seamless transition. We were all taken aback by the way the instructional team had begun to relate to each other. I left Main Street School with a desire to return to Orange School District.

CHAPTER TWO

You have to take risks and understand that some will result in failure.

—Grace Sammon

Orange Middle School

Small Learning Communities—
Creating a Nurturing Environment

In October 2005, the following year, I was asked to be the interim principal of Orange Middle School (OMS). Orange Middle School had an enrollment of approximately eight hundred seventh—and eighth-grade students and a teaching staff of approximately seventy teachers. The school was housed in what was formerly Orange High School. In 1974, with all the charm of a midcentury brick edifice, it became Orange Middle School. Although OMS had quite the reputation, I was interested in this assignment. The story that reverberated in my mind was "I would never send my child to that school." At this juncture, I knew that I had turned two schools around, and I felt comfortable with this challenge. At 11:00 a.m. on my first day at OMS, the superintendent of schools introduced me to the two assistant principals and returned to his office. Immediately after his departure, I went from classroom to classroom, introducing myself to each teacher, staff member, and the students. If a teacher was out at the time of my introductions, I revisited that teacher later. Approximately four hours later, the superintendent returned for a faculty meeting, and he offered an update on the "principal's search," and a staff member quickly responded, "Why can't Dr. Kronin be our principal?" The superintendent responded, "You just met her four hours ago." Thus, the most important position in my career began to evolve. My past professional experience and the day-to-day efforts by the staff under my instructional leadership was enough to enable me to be appointed principal of Orange Middle School in February of 2006.

Like many middle schools in urban settings, Orange Middle School fell short of its potential. It was affected by low scores in core subjects, an unsettling climate that included many of the urban nightmares—students in halls instead of classrooms, gang issues, significant ESL-bilingual and special education populations, limited parent involvement, and a lack of central focus. Not long after I arrived, we addressed each area of concern. The first initiative was to let the faculty know that I had the utmost respect for them. I was struck by their willingness to go above and beyond their realm of responsibility, a sign of who they were. We created open lines of communication and dialogued about "good instruction."

The staff and I revisited the discipline code and decided that there would not be any exceptions to any rules. All students were treated respectfully, and we let them know that they were our clients and without them, we would not have a school. Students who were chronically disruptive were educated in a nontraditional setting that offered greater structure. Orange Public School District had an operational alternative program for students for grades 7 through 12. Fourteen students were assigned to this program. Discipline improved, and this program was returned to its normal enrollment the following year.

Over the span of a year, OMS transitioned into five thematically-based small learning communities (SLCs)—law, health sciences, math and technology, visual arts, and performing arts or prodigy hall.

This initiative was the vision of Sam Hazel, the former principal of Orange High School, and was supported by Dr. Nathan Parker, superintendent, and members of central office. The model for this program was the brainchild of the Bill Gates Institute for Research and Reform in Education (IRRE), which was appropriately referred to as First Things First. It was designed to be a secondary initiative and, therefore, included Main Street School and Orange High.

Although there is a preponderance of research on the value and the use of the small learning communities model, Klem (2009) and Connell (2004) emphasized their connection to high standards. Conditions include high standards for academic learning and conduct, meaningful and engaging pedagogy and curriculum, professional learning communities among staff, and personalized learning environments. Schools providing such support are more likely to have students who are engaged and connected to the school.

The implementation at OMS required an aggressive but orderly plan for transitioning from a middle school model into a small learning communities model (SLCM). Central office staff members supported every phase of the transition. This included providing coverage for teachers when they participated in professional development training of each component of the model.

OMS staff understood that the goal of the SLCM initiative was to create a focused thematic-based curriculum that afforded students easy access to their teachers in five nurturing, cohesive small "family-like settings."

Although the schedule was extremely demanding, the OMS staff managed to meet the high demands of this schedule. Student and staff surveys designed by First Things First were used to determine the themes of the SLCM; planning and training sessions were scheduled for the staff to learn the roles and responsibilities for the new positions of this model. The SLC coordinator and school facilitator, the common planning period, and family advocacy were the key new positions and components of our SLCM. That year, 2005-2006, the staff met two sets of professional responsibilities, one which required us to address the day-to-day operations and the other, which required us to plan, acquire the training to execute the tasks for the successful transition into the SLCM for the following year.

The goal was to open the 2006-2007 school year as a learning center comprised of the five designated SLCs. Elections were held for the appointment of coordinators for each of the five SLCs. Each SLC coordinator was elected unopposed.

With a coordinator supervising each SLC team, the organizational structure was designed to empower teachers. This paradigm shift was clearly articulated, and the instructional team was prepared to assume extensive decision-making responsibilities. The staff engaged in extensive discussions to clarify their expanded decision-making responsibilities in both the area of instruction and student discipline. Each SLC included approximately 125 seventh—and eighth-grade students, and each had a teaching staff of two math teachers, two language arts teachers, a social studies teacher, and a science teacher. Elective teachers were shared across the communities.

The school facilitator scheduled all staff and student meetings, (1) disaggregated analyzed and interpreted data, (2) attended the common planning meetings of each SLC, (3) scheduled all professional development training, and (4) reported all pertinent matters directly to the principal. In addition to all the usual professional responsibilities that they normally assumed, the two assistant principals, the two guidance counselors, and the principal also assumed the role and responsibility as the facilitator for one of the SLCs.

At the end of the school year, after the students were dismissed for the summer vacation, the building administrative team reserved a half day on the school calendar for the OMS staff to transition from the former OMS organizational model to the new SLCM with the new roles and responsibilities. The event focused on the actual physical movement by team members of each of the five new SLCs to their newly designated areas of our building. It was the birth of the Orange Middle School small learning communities: health sciences, law and order, technology-math, visual arts, and performing arts. This was the first time that SLCs met as teams at their new locations. It was a history-making moment, and the staff felt a huge sense of accomplishment. Accordingly, Dr. Michelle Fine of the City University of New York Graduate Center stated, "Small Learning communities are the single most powerful intervention for young people." We accomplished our goal; we had completed our transformation and were prepared for a great 2006-2007school year. We celebrated with cake, punch, and congratulatory hugs. We left for summer vacation with the belief that we had begun the journey of establishing an educational program that had high expectations for our students.

Education is the ability to listen to almost anything without losing your temper and your self confidence.

—Robert Frost

Bumps along the Way

Of course, the transition into SLCM came about with the normal number of pitfalls. In addition to the 10 percent of the staff who constantly complained about everything associated with SLCM, we had a few major setbacks. Although we had fewer incidents of student disruptions, after each one, we would hear, "This program is not working." This comment was prevalent during our transition, prior to the implementation date of the model, and during the early stages of implementation. This frustration peaked at one of our faculty meetings.

Typically, our faculty meetings were conducted three times a month, immediately after student dismissal, in the cafeteria. At one of these faculty meetings, the entire staff entered the meeting and made an about-face and remained facing the four walls of the cafeteria for the entire meeting. Their actions were a reflection of the pressures related to the many impending deadlines that we faced during the process. Although the agenda of this particular faculty meeting included a number of time-sensitive initiatives, the reality of the situation was, the meeting was not going to happen that day. I also knew I could not overreact. My response to the staff was to acknowledge the stress that we were all experiencing from the strenuous tasks associated with the implementation process of the SLCM, which involved all the normal responsibilities and a new set of unfamiliar responsibilities associated with the SLCM. I assured the staff that the administrative team was open to listening to their concerns and developing some resolutions to resolve these issues to the best of our abilities. I concluded the meeting with a little levity; "With your backs against the wall, I bid you good night." Of course, that matter was discussed at length and resolved. Sometimes staff members need to know that they are being considered and respected. It was a clear message to the administrative team that we needed to slow down and make sure that everyone was on board and comfortable with the initiative and the related tasks.

On another occasion, a staff member disrupted a professional development workshop, which was being facilitated by an IRRE staff member. My administrative team agreed that our initial steps for resolving the faculty meeting incident would be to attain an accurate reading of the staff's concerns. The investigation taught us several lessons, including the following: misinformation is transmitted as quickly as accurate information, and information must be communicated using several different forms of communication, and each one has to be repeated several times. Important information, involving the implementation of SLCs, had to be (1)discussed at staff meetings, (2) sent out electronically, (3) placed in every teacher's mailbox (hard copy), and then (4) this same information had to be discussed in small group settings and discussed with particular individuals in the building (union representative, facilitator, guidance counselors, literacy and math coaches.) The staff became familiar with this information protocol. Often my memos would cross-reference previous memos. This minimized the miscommunication and reduced the likelihood that our professional efforts would not be compromised. Every effort was put in place for the staff to refocus on our SLC mission. When it was all said and done, even though we thought we were doing an effective job, my administrative team had to demonstrate that we were willing to listen more to our staff and offer them greater respect.

Both incidents were resolved by collaborating with the Orange Education Association (OEA). OEA had a reputation of being fair, and in the case of the huge SLC undertaking, we often leaned on each other's shoulders. Early on in my administrative career, I learned the importance of honoring all personnel contracts and never attempting the implementation of any initiative without a sit-down, face-to-face meeting with the president of the teachers association and the building representative of the teachers association. This practice was followed even in situations that obviously benefited teachers.

Our administrative team set high standards for our staff. Everyone was held accountable for meeting their professional responsibilities. Defiance and willful behavior were not tolerated, and while we were never sought revenge, we never allowed any staff member to disrupt our efforts to improve the instructional program for our students. We firmly believed that our students deserved to have an exemplary educational program, one that was on par with the best schools in the country. Needless to say, all staff members did not survive our rigorous mission.

It's our choices that show who we truly are, far more than our abilities.

—John Dewey

Orange Education Association

As I reflect back on the design of SLCM, the first major hurdle that had to be tackled with the district and the OEA was family advocacy, which is the advisory component of the SLCM. Although as the principal of Orange Middle School, I did not attend any of these meetings, I knew it was a tough sell to convince the OEA president to have the membership take on an additional assignment. After a considerable amount of going back and forth, a compromise was reached, and all secondary schools in Orange had a family advocacy component as part of the SLCM. I was very proud of my relationship with all staff members in Orange Public School District; I was particularly pleased with the actions of OEA on this important initiative. Although on many occasions, I sat opposite the president and the vice president as they represented their constituency, I always felt they considered the impact that our decisions would have on our students. It was not unusual for my building administration and the OEA executive board to come together to attain a win-win resolution for the teachers and/or students involved in cases. This practice of collaboratively reaching agreements where all parties mutually agreed often enabled the district to remain focused on the goal of improving classroom instruction. As I compare my past administrative experiences in other school districts, this type of mutual respect between the teachers' association and the administration did not exist, and this single factor was extremely detrimental to school reform.

Most staff members throughout Orange District had a "we are all in this together attitude," and this included the OEA executive board and members. This pleasantry extended to social events. The OEA president and vice president fought very hard for their constituency; but administrators could expect them to be equally supportive of students. This is not to say that we did not haggle over contracts and that these matters sometimes escalated to arbitration. But when it came to doing the right thing for our students, it was a case of solidarity. The year after the implementation of the First Things First small learning communities model, staff from all three secondary schools in Orange and the OEA executive board boarded a plane and attended the First Things First Conference in Phoenix, Arizona. There, we reflected upon the crests and valleys involved with the implementation of SLCM, developed a plan for improvement, and enjoyed each others' company.

The great aim of education is not knowledge but action.

—Herbert Spencer

Orange Middle School Small Learning Communities

When Orange Middle School opened its doors on September 2006, it was difficult for the staff to contain their excitement. The school had transitioned from a traditional middle school model into a SLCM. The students followed an alternating A Day-B Day schedule with two daily blocks of language arts and math and one block of social studies, science, and physical education. All students in each of the SLCs followed this generic schedule. Each block was equivalent to eighty-two minutes. The elective subjects were art, music, and dance and were offered for forty minutes on alternating days. The students looked marvelous on opening day. The entire population of seventh and eighth graders was required to follow a dress of white collared shirts and khaki pants/skirts. Glancing over the sea of students as they sat in the auditorium, the visual could be compared to a scene from a prestigious prep school. The traditional visit by members of the Orange Board of Education was profoundly different from other first-day-of-school visits. The administrative team knew that this was a new beginning, and our school was forever changed.

When OMS transformed into the SLCM of five mini schools within a large school, the change in the dynamics was astonishing. Each SLC took on a personality of its own and began to perform as high-performing teams.

Prodigy Hall Performing Arts was the most disciplined of all the SLCs. Few, if any, students reported to school without proper dress attire, the white shirt (blouse) with a collar and khaki slacks (skirt); and if they did, the faculty team members created a set of rules that discouraged this behavior. They had a powerful reward system and consequences for not meeting the established expectations. They presented outstanding performances, which were extremely innovative for the school and the community.

<u>Prodigy Hall Performing Arts Community</u>

- Participating in productions on a professional level, self-actualizing the life and responsibilities of young artists.
- Performing with band, chorus, drama club, or dance ensemble.
- Writing scripts and lyrics.
- Applying make-up, planning choreography and costume design.
- Directing and producing shows.
- Producing and recording music.
- Participating in the stage crew: managing props, equalizing sound boards, coordinating light cues, etc.
- Learning marketing and promotional tactics while recruiting audiences.

The Technology SLC developed a reputation for earning the highest scores on state assessments in language arts and formed a very cohesive team. These students gained insight into how mathematics is used as a universal language through technological mediums such as web authoring, podcasting, and Excel processing.

<u>Technology & Mathematics Community</u>

- In Tech-Math, students will be able to integrate mathematics into technology.
- Students will have an understanding of how mathematics is used as an universal language through technological mediums such as Web Authoring, Podcasting, and Excel Processing.
- Student will have the opportunity to problem solve mathematically with technology.
- Student will be able to explore Careers in technology development from video games to software engineering.

The Health Sciences SLC was highly competitive and had the distinctive reputation of having a student who earned a perfect score on the math portion of the NJ ASK 7. Their students also earned the highest percentage of proficient and advanced-proficient scores on the state assessment in science. This SLC is dedicated to practicing healthy habits in order to promote healthy citizenship.

Health/Science Community

- This small learning community offers a well-rounded, interdisciplinary approach to students who are interested in sports medicine, health, nutrition and natural sciences (biology, botany, and environmental science).
- This community is dedicated to practicing healthy habits in order to promote healthy citizenship.
- The Health Sciences Community implements a new crossdisciplined, project-

The Visual Arts SLC was highly competitive and earned the distinct recognition for their academic achievement. They inspired their students to design award-winning projects in science and other core subjects. This SLC provided an intimate and stimulating learning environment where students communicated ideas and experiences through their artistic and visual skills while preparing for their future.

Visual Arts Community

- The Visual Arts Community provides an intimate and stimulating learning environment where students can communicate ideas and experiences through their artistic and visual skills while preparing them with the core knowleged needed for high school, college, and future careers.

- Students will learn to communicate their ideas and experiences through visuals?

- Students will use images, pictures, colors, and maps to organize information and communicate with others.

- Example of this process that the student used visual learning of objects, plans, and outcomes is through a media called "Podcasting."

  - A podcast is a digital media file or collection of filles that is distributed over the internet. The files can then be played back on a computer or personal player (eg, an Ipod). The method by which podcasts are distributed is often called podcasting.

The law community established a reputation for developing students who had expert skills of US Constitution and constitutional law.

Their members often represented OMS at regional and state events and conferences related to law. It was common knowledge that the SLCs were on par with each other since there were only two requests to transfer from one SLC to another by students or teachers. The transformation in the SLCM was such a success that OMS often received requests from other middle schools to tour our program. Administrators from other schools visited and conferred to learn techniques and procedures that could be followed for implementation of our small learning communities model.

An understanding heart is everything in a teacher and cannot be esteemed highly enough. One looks back with appreciation to the brilliant teachers, but with gratitude to those who touched our human feeling. The curriculum is so much necessary raw material, but warmth is the vital element the growing plant and for the soul of the child.

—Carl Gustav Jung

Family Advocacy

One day a week, all schedules of secondary schools in the district were adjusted to include forty minutes of family advocacy. This important component was designed so every secondary student in the district had an advocate. Every member of the instructional team met with eight to ten students of their SLC. The role of the family advocate was that of a support person for their students. Each had the responsibility of monitoring their students' academic performance and to communicate twice per month with the parents and/or guardians of their students. The family advocates were given a huge binder of curriculum activities that were specially designed to enhance character development and self-esteem. This binder was created and designed by IRRE's First Things First. A significant portion of the 2007-2008 opening school year staff development was devoted to a workshop, which enabled the instructional staff to become familiar with the family advocacy activities in this binder.

At OMS, the administrators, SCL facilitator, and the SLC coordinator worked diligently to make sure that this program ran effectively, our students benefitted. It was common practice to find all administrators, the school facilitator, and the guidance counselors sweeping the halls on Thursdays, at 2:00 p.m., the day and time at OMS that was designated for family advocacy. Sweeping the halls refers to the practice of making sure all students are in their assigned classes, and in this particular case, family advocacy.

Our data indicated that the program had wide student and parental appeal. The parents cited that this program enabled them to have a clearer insight into the activities that their children were involved in and afforded them greater access to their teachers. Parents now had a choice of communicating with their child's guidance counselor or their family advocate. Often the child had a closer relationship with their family advocate than with their guidance counselor. Good family advocates became an invaluable resource to parents.

It was not uncommon for a parent to call a family advocate to inquire about a concern they were having with their child. These phone calls often led to an invitation by the SLC to meet with all their child's teachers.

When teachers had problems with their students, they often met with the student's family advocate to gain greater insight. Sometimes this resulted in the teacher attaining advice on how to handle a particular problem or the family advocate having an individual conference with the student.

Family advocacy was an important factor for improving the school climate at OMS and in the district. After the implementation of this program, the number of incidents of violence and vandalism declined significantly. The yearly statistics recorded in the Violence and Vandalism Report support the observation that our school climate improved.

I personally looked forward to meeting with my family advocate students. This was an opportunity to bond with a group of students attending my school in a way that would not have been possible without our weekly meetings. I often readjusted my schedule to avoid missing family advocacy. I made members of the cabinet and parents aware that I was not available during family advocacy time.

I shared my responsibilities of family advocacy with Ms. Denise Wynn, our language arts coach. She is one of the smartest professionals that I have ever encountered. She is an ideal professional: she was highly talented, well organized, prepared; and she related extremely well to these students. It was a pleasure to share my responsibilities with her. I learned so much from her, and I treasure the time that we spent with our student advocates. We were a good balance for each other; she tended to monitor the students' grades while I had a tendency to engage the students, giving them opportunities to express their point of view and perspective. She concentrated on the students' work habits, which enabled the students to improve their relationship with their teachers. I offered a balance to this by encouraging the students to engage in relevant discussions relating to political, economic, cultural, local, and/or state issues.

Bonding with my advocates enabled me to view OMS through the eyes of innocent seventh and eighth graders. The diverse backgrounds made each meeting a unique exchange of ideas and cultures.

A young man of Haitian heritage, who spoke fluent English, became the voice for another Haitian student who only spoke French Creole. The latter student seldom uttered a word to anyone other than his fellow compatriot. After one year, this student found his comfort zone.

A young Nigerian student, who had recently come to the United States without her parents, often entertained us by singing original Nigerian compositions, allowing us to make interesting comparisons between Nigerian culture and our culture.

Another student with an exciting and charming personality often had our group on high alert as a result of his day-to-day encounters with his teachers and his peers. Further, a young lady from El Salvador delighted us with stories of her country. Although she only spoke Spanish, she went to great lengths to motivate us to learn her language while she tackled English.

The final member of our group was a young lady who fought feverishly to the objections of her parents to participate in extracurricular activities. She achieved honor roll status because of her belief of high expectations. She designed projects that truly challenged her critical thinking skills. She shared with the group the technique that she used to learn to speak Japanese via television.

We had interesting discussions and projects during our sessions, which included following the Democratic and Republican primaries. The students became familiar with the platforms of each of the candidates, and they were able to offer intelligent comments on day-to-day issues. Their views and perspectives were posted, and interesting debates followed along with conversations regarding the candidates' qualifications and their entanglements along the campaign trail. It became clear that the students' views and opinions were influenced by what they saw on TV, read in the newspaper, and discussed in their homes.

Family advocacy was sacred time, and the advocates enjoyed being with their students as much as the students enjoyed being with them. The small cozy settings became excellent forums for the students to develop social skills. The students learned how to listen as others spoke during discussions or debates, and they learned the importance of tolerance and being civil to each other. This came about naturally by setting a tone of mutual respect. In our particular family advocacy group, we never had any incidents of disruptions; and while there were incidents of disruptions from time to time during family advocacy, they were minimal.

An equal amount of time was devoted to discussions related to the students' academic progress. Since students in each advocacy group had the same teachers and were in many of the same classes, advocates were able to have rich, in-depth conversations about their students' study habits and classroom behavior. In the case of our particular group, it wasn't long before we knew our students' academic strengths and weaknesses. We zeroed in on our students' organizational skills. One of the challenges faced by the students involved the organization of their homework assignments for each course that they took. This issue was compounded by the A Day-B Day schedule. One strategy that was employed was to assist them in organizing their book bags. This was a particular concern for many of the boys; they often tossed completed assignments in their book bags haphazardly and then were unable to find and submit them to their teachers to be graded. This was interesting because often their parents emphatically responded to their teachers, telling them that they had watched their children complete homework assignments and they became confused when their child's teacher complained that these assignments were never turned in. Family advocates got to the root cause of these types of problems, which seem obvious to adults but were dilemmas for seventh—and eighth-grade students.

Through experience and conversation, advocates quickly learned of the severity of the impact of the students' limited interpersonal skills on their academic growth. Numerous incidents relating to students' inability to relate well with their teachers were reported. The resolution to these dilemmas was to engage students in activities that developed better communication skills. As students acquired communication skills, related issues began to be addressed, in particular, the reoccurring situations that involved students with faltering relationships with their teachers. The goal was to consciously help students become more tolerant of the diverse world that they inhabited. Students were taught to employ civility in their interactions and particularly those that involved their teachers. This task was challenging, given the admission that this was not only difficult for students to master, but was also challenging for some of their teachers. Often, discussions on this topic began initially by encouraging students to understand their inner voice, meaning their position on popular social, political, religious, or economic issues. The advocates noticed that when students engaged in rich discussions, they gained insight into their understanding of their personal perspective as they related to their liberal, moderate, conservative, or independent viewpoints. Like many of their teachers, they recognized that their views varied on certain issues and were firm on others. They began to understand what it takes to change their opinion or the opinion of others on an issue. Advocates began to see conversations evolve from objective, shallow chatter to rich conversations. They witnessed fewer inappropriate remarks, which were typical and expedient responses, when students encountered opposing viewpoints. The advocates observed an increased number of responses that began with quiet introspection, indicating that students were engaged in reflection and taking time to articulate an opinion before they spoke. Students learned to value wait time and became good listeners. It became common practice for students to take time to hear what the other person was saying. The result was rich conversations and fewer conversations going awry because one party exclusively focused on what they were about to say and failed to listen to what is being said. Most importantly, the students learned how to disagree without being disagreeable. The training also included the importance of respecting authority figures, which included parents, teachers, administrators, other adults. Time and attention was devoted to thinking before speaking and the value of giving oneself wait time, and lastly, we stressed the importance of speaking with a voice that was not influenced by peer pressure but truly reflected the students' point of view even if it was not popular. Students were encouraged to take positions based upon their point of view as it relates to religion, politics, economy, culture, education, passion, and common sense. Eventually, this same set of skills was integrated in their problem-solving techniques.

We learned of the horrific conditions that family advocate students operated under: an honor student's mom was incarcerated and, therefore, missed the student's eighth graduation program; another student did not have a winter coat; one student with a speech impediment chose to participate in the production of *The Twelfth Night*; and another student reported incidents of child abuse.

In my family advocacy group, we honored the student who only spoke Creole and chose to communicate only with another Haitian student. The following year, when I became interim superintendent of the district, this same young man who I believed received the least benefit from our discussions sent me a card in English that moved me to tears. He wrote that he missed family advocacy and that he had learned more at

OMS than he had ever learned in his entire life. This had an amazing impact upon me. I suddenly appreciated my knowledge of Gardner's theory of multiple intelligences and learning styles. "Students possess different mindsets and therefore learn, remember, perform and understand in different ways" (Gardner, 1991). Although this young man did not engage in any of the verbal exchanges with the other students or teachers, this was not evidence that he was not learning. In fact, contrary to this belief, his style of learning is what Gardner refers to as a solitary learner.

After receiving this card from this student, I stopped by his class to thank him, we had a lengthy conversation, and I saw evidence that he was positively affected by family advocacy. I watched as he displayed confidence; he shared his educational goals and his personal career plans with me. Similarly, the other students from my family advocacy group were doing equally well. Their growth was amazing.

Education is what survives when what has been learned has been forgotten.

—B. F. Skinner

Orange Middle School

Report Card Narrative: NJDOE

2008-2009 School Year

It is significant that Orange Middle School continues to utilize the small learning communities model as the school organizational model. The report states,

Exemplary Programs

Orange Middle School continued to implement small learning communities—health sciences, visual arts, technology-math, law, and prodigy hall. Students selected a community based on their preferred learning styles and interests. Each small learning community developed thematic interdisciplinary projects/units, based on NJCCCS, in order to demonstrate the relationships between subjects. Additionally, each certified staff member was assigned approximately ten students for family advocacy. Once a week, the advocate and students met to discuss school issues, study habits, grades, and interpersonal relationships. The advocate also met with students individually and had contact with the parents at least once per month. Job-embedded professional learning emphasized guided reading, coteaching, data-driven instruction, and universal design learning in ELL classes. Data from Learnia and DRA2 was utilized to differentiate instruction. Cooperative learning groups, learning stations, Socratic questioning, and accountable talk continued to be implemented in order to raise student achievement.

Student Activities

Orange Middle School offered before-school, after-school, and Saturday programs. The Homework Center, Cyber Café, Bilingual Tutorial, and the Breakfast Club met at 7:30 a.m. After-school clubs included Chess Club, Guitar Club, Art Club, Female Achievers, Dance Ensemble, Chorus, LAL Remediation Center, Math Remediation Center, Science Remediation Center, Sisterhood, Peer Leadership/Student Council, Memory Book Club, Soccer, Intramural Sports, Drama Club, and Concert Band. On Saturdays, the NJ ASK special education tutorial and NJ ASK prep were held.

Parent Participation

Parent participation on the School Leadership Council continued to play an important role in program planning and budget decision making. Additionally, family advocacy closed the communication gap between home and school. Our precollege night provided parents and students with information from local colleges and personal experiences from Orange Middle School students who are enrolled in colleges both in and out of New Jersey. The SEEDS orientation program was very well attended and provided parents with information for this partnership program. The literacy coach and the mathematics coach provided parents with information on the school's programs and the NJ ASK objectives.

Special Staff and/or Student Achievement

Several students earned first-place honors in county and regional essay contests. Fifteen students were accepted into the NJ SEEDS College Preparatory Program. Our dance ensemble took gold medal honors at the regional Starbound National Dance Competition and participated in the nationals. The Drama Club won accolades at the Drew University New Jersey Shakespeare Theatre competition. Fourteen eighth graders took the PSAT. Excellent thematic projects were created by each small learning community including Everybody Counts, The Last Lecture: Achieving Your Dreams, Election Law, Guilty or Not, Our Civic Responsibility, Adaptations in Natural Law, Orange Goes Green, Heroes, Out of this World, The History of Orange Middle School, Election 2008, Global Warming, Distance Learning, the Role of Universal Health Care Platforms in the 2008 Elections, and Changes We Need for the 21st Century. The five SLCs took twenty-six exciting field trips that related directly to the students' courses of study.

The best teacher is the one who suggests rather than dogmatizes, and inspires his listener with the wish to teach himself.

—Edward Bulwer-Lytton

The Benefits of Small Learning Communities

The teachers and students agree that OMS benefited from the small learning community model. The schedules of both the students and the teachers allowed for greater interaction. Having five SLCs in specified locations within a larger unit have some distinct advantages in any setting, and this was true at OMS. Immediately after the implementation of the SLC, students reported that they felt safer; and consequently, the academic achievement and behavior of students in all the SLCs improved. The impact of this nurturing environment also improved the percentage of students who met the state requirements for the completion of eighth-grade requirements. The failure of a large number of eighth-grade students was the major cause for the disruptive atmosphere that plagued the school when I arrived at the school as the instructional leader in 2005. Prior to the implementation of SLCM, the large organizational structure added to the serious problems associated with a disruptive school climate.

Another major advantage was, students were now able to take advanced courses. The first year that OMS implemented the SLCM, four eighth-grade students were recommended to enroll in algebra, a ninth-grade course at Orange High School. The following year, the instructional staff designed an honors program.

This honors program was designed for each of the five SLCs to have one section of honors classes for seventh-grade students and one section for eighth-grade students. The criteria were the same for all SLC students. Students had to maintain a grade-point average of B+, complete all homework assignments, and display high standards of citizenship. In the first year of this program, all students took ninth-grade algebra; and in the second year, they took algebra and biology, two ninth-grade subjects. This meant the honor students had to meet all eighth-grade requirements and the requirements of two ninth-grade courses.

Another distinct advantage of the OMS-SLCM was a dramatic increase in student participation in extracurricular activities. There was an increase in the number of offerings of extracurricular activities as well as in student participation. In a very short amount of time, OMS became highly competitive in academic subjects as well as the arts. Orange Dance Ensemble, Guitar Club, Chess Club, Art Club, Concert Band, and Female Achievers were among the clubs and programs that flourished.

The true spirit of conversation consists in building on another man's
observation not, overturning it.

—Edward Bulwer-Lytton

Common Planning Meetings

The common planning meetings (CPM) were a great benefit to both the teachers and students of SLCs. Twice per week, each SLC had an opportunity to meet as an SLC team. Eventually, they began to serve as a powerful tool for school reform and a major resource for improving classroom instruction.

Prior to the inclusion of common planning time into teachers' schedules, our teachers reported that they felt isolated from each other. They complained that they didn't have opportunities to share ideas, knowledge, or visit each others' classrooms. The flexibility of the SLC schedule made it possible for teachers to have opportunities for professional interactions throughout the regular school day. In the past, many of our staff who attended professional development on topics of instructional strategies had little opportunities to discuss their professional learning with their colleagues, and in many instances, they had little support or motivation for implementation of these instructional strategies. Some staff members viewed professional-development days as a break from the overwhelming routine of working in isolation with little instructional support. Some teachers viewed their classrooms as their private domains and did not expect anyone to enter other than their students. This was part of the belief system of veteran teachers, and their expectations were minimal classroom visits, which included only one formal observation. This was reinforced by the common practice of administrators who seldom visited classrooms unless there was a student or teacher infraction. A visit by an administrator was associated with negativity and not as an opportunity to improve instruction or an opportunity to model good instruction. There was little incentive to improve instruction, and good instruction was seldom discussed. An inordinate amount of time was devoted to discipline, and very seldom did anyone link or articulate positive classroom climate to good instruction. Very few instructional leaders offered instructional strategies to teachers they considered poor disciplinarians. Common planning meetings afforded teachers who fell short in this category an opportunity to model best practices from members of their team in a supportive setting.

Members of each SLC collectively decided on the instructional strategies that they would use to teach each unit. The interdisciplinary approach meant each member had collaborative responsibilities to the team. Failure to meet one's professional responsibilities put the entire team at risk. On the other hand, if a colleague needed help, he or she had an entire team ready to support that person. There was only one occasion that team members requested that a teacher be removed from an SLC. If an administrator observed a classroom strategy that needed attention, it was discussed with the SCL facilitator and team leader, and together, they could provide assistance for the teacher.

The implementation of CPM changed the mind-set that seeking assistance was a sign of weakness. These meetings were designed to improve student achievement. With the assistance of the administrative team, the school facilitator, the SLC coordinators, the team members of each SLC became responsible for planning and conducting the biweekly CPM. Further, the members of each SLC began to appreciate the degree of empowerment that accompanied the new organizational structure, and an important goal was achieved. Teachers learned to function as members of instructional teams.

OMS was extremely fortunate. With very few exceptions, the instructional staff took the high road and accepted their new roles and responsibilities. The administrative team employed a check-and-balance system to monitor the progress that was being achieved.

The agenda items of the CPM included classroom instruction, student work, and student progress. Discussions on classroom instruction began with the instructional goal of creating interdisciplinary thematic units. Using the New Jersey Core Curriculum Content Standards (NJCCCS) for each of the core subjects, language arts, math, science, and social studies, each SLC developed thematic units related to their themes of each SLC, which included performing arts, health sciences, visual arts, technology-math, and law and order.

A significant portion of the CPM was devoted to conversations regarding student progress. Meaningful discussions frequently occurred with the members of SLC at CPM since they had a common set of students. By sharing conversations about the strengths and weaknesses of their students, they became aware of the different learning styles of their students. Eventually, this led to improved and optimal academic performance of a significant number of their students.

Also, learning from each other what their students liked/disliked and insights into the students' family culture often gave teachers insight into developing rapport with students that they had not been able to previously reach. This practice was further enhanced by sharing information learned from family advocacy meetings. They also learned that the close relationships developed during family advocacy could help their colleagues with students who act out in class.

Initially, the greatest portion of CPM was devoted to discussing the behavior of students. Although the administrative team knew that many of the classroom behavior problems would be resolved when the instructional team improved the delivery of instruction in our classrooms, we also knew that the instructional team had to come to this realization on their own. OMS, like all schools, had pockets of good teachers;

and therefore, good instruction was only taking place in some of the classrooms, some of the time.

Instruction began to improve when the administrative team began initiating conversations about the good instruction that was being observed and by listening very carefully to the teachers' instructional concerns.

The SLC coordinators were requested to make a concerted effort to shift the conversations and discussions at CPM from discipline to instruction. The administrative team encouraged SLC coordinators, the SLC facilitator, and team members of each SLC to have discussions at CPM, which involved the development of strategies that created opportunities for meaningful student participation and strategies that inspired students to take responsibility for their learning. The administrative team had real concerns that the OMS instructional staff was using traditional teaching strategies in a nontraditional model, and consequently, it was not working. Common planning time was an excellent vehicle for improving classroom instruction. However, improved classroom instruction was only going to happen if the administrative team provided instructional coaching.

The mediocre teacher tells. The good teacher explains. The superior teacher demonstrates. The great teacher inspires.

—William Arthur Ward

Improving Classroom Instruction

The administrative team at OMS comprised of two assistant principals and a principal, who listened carefully to the comments that were made about school operations. This included comments that related to how teachers felt about the SLCM and what they believed the administrative team needed to do to address the behavior of our students. We agreed with much of what they said.

The administrative team decided to start this major instructional initiative by visiting classrooms as a team, and each visit would be followed by a debriefing meeting. After a few visits and debriefing sessions, we were able to articulate some of our observations to the instructional staff. Our approach was to cite best instructional practices and share what we had observed. Detailed memos were written, which were designed for the staff to use as a guide for professional improvement. Through consistency, we began to establish common language.

The entire instructional team agreed on a list of items that were expected to be visible and available in all classrooms. We referred to these items as the non-negotiable list. At faculty meetings, we often used the cooperative learning group model (CLGM) for professional learning activities. Each of the five SLCs separated into CLGs, and each created a list of instructional items that they believed should be part of the instructional environment in all classrooms at OMS. The designated presenter shared their findings. The resulting lists from each of the SLCs were very similar. The administrative team refined the lists by comparing them to a list issued by the New Jersey Department of Education (NJDOE). This became our list of non-negotiable items.

When the administrative team walked into a classroom at OMS, we expected all teachers to have their name and lesson objectives on the board, NJCCCS, lesson plan visibly on the teacher's desk, a word wall, relevant bulletin boards, rubrics related to the subject being taught, student portfolios, and a display of student work that was graded using rubrics and a clutter-free environment. This was an important standard at OMS. It gave anyone visiting a classroom at OMS evidence that the instructional team was meeting the standards set by the NJDOE.

The administrative team started to have meaningful discussions with the instructional staff and with each teacher who did not understand the outlined expectations. The administrative team went out of its way to make sure that teachers knew our visits were for the purpose of improving classroom instruction for students and to improve their level of professionalism.

The next phase of our instructional initiative was to identify best instructional practices, which could improve instruction across the board. The administrative team visited classrooms to observe and identify the instructional practices that encouraged students to engage in critical thinking. We listened carefully to the conversations that teachers were sharing about instructional practices that they believed worked.

We visited classrooms with the mind-set that we were learning valuable information about the instructional practices of our staff, those that were effective and those that were not. The findings were, (1) there were pockets of excellent teaching throughout each SLC; (2) the teachers who consistently handed in well-designed instructional lesson plans were the same teachers who delivered the most effective classroom instruction; (3) the students of teachers whose practices were based upon a constructivist approach had a high percentage of students who engaged in critical thinking; (4) teachers who based their practices upon the behaviorist approach had a high percentage of their students engage in objective or rote learning; (5) teachers who were least prepared encountered the greatest number of discipline problems; (6) students learned more when they were given opportunities to problem-solve;(7) there was limited student participation when teachers designed lecture-styled instructional lessons; (8) classroom rigor was not prevalent in many of the classrooms that were visited; (9) teachers did not ask enough Socratic questions; (10) in some classes, instructional practices worked well for some students and not well for other students; some teachers did not understand how to make optimal use out of their instructional time, which was eighty-two minutes per instructional block; and (11) many teachers did not understand how to make smooth transitions from one instructional activity to the next.

The administrative team identified the need for an instructional model that could enable our students to become critical thinkers and independent learners. Our goal was to raise the level of academic achievement by creating a joy of teaching and learning. The literature and research that we reviewed included Tomlison, A. (1995); Forsten, C., Grant, J., and Hollas, B. (2002); Skinner, B. F. (1984); Fosnot, C. (1996); and Stahl, R. J. (1994). We familiarized ourselves with the appropriate application of learning theories, differentiated instruction for the diverse populations and inclusion classrooms that included special education students, the Socratic method for improving teachers' questioning techniques, and cooperative learning groups to encourage students to take responsibility for their learning.

Our findings included the following:

- Differentiated instruction, at its most basic level, is defined as the efforts of teachers to respond to variances among learners in a classroom; and whenever a teacher reaches out to an individual or small group to vary his or her teaching in order to create the best learning experience possible, that teacher is differentiating instruction. (Tomlinson, C., 1995)

- Teachers can differentiate four classroom elements based on student readiness or learning profile: (1) content—meaning what the student needs to learn or how the student will get access to information, (2) process—meaning the activities in which the student engages in order to make sense of or master the content, (3) products—meaning culminating projects that asks the student to rehearse, apply, and extend what he or she has learned in a unit, and (4) environment—meaning the way the classroom works and feels. (Tomlinson, C., 1995)

- Psychologists tell us that students learn only when the task is a little too hard for that student. When the student can do the work with little effort and virtually independently, that student is not learning but rather rehearsing the known. Further, when a student finds a task beyond his or her reach, frustration, no learning is the result. Forsten emphasized only when a task is a *bit* beyond the student's comfort level and the student finds a support system to bridge the gap does learning occur. According to Forsten, this optimum degree of difficulty for learning is referred for learning to as *the student's zone of proximal development.* (Forsten, C., 2002)

- We reminded our instructional staff of the importance of using common planning meetings as a resource for improving instruction and reducing teacher isolation. Carroll and Fulton (2004) make reference to the seriousness of this issue. Nearly 540,000 teachers moved to other schools or left the teaching profession in 2000—many of them due to feelings of isolation. Despite the investment they had made of four, sometimes five, years of their time and money in college education, spending hundreds of hours obtaining a job in a very competitive field, 46 percent of new teachers nationwide leave the profession within the first five years of service. (Ingersoll, 2002)

The administrative team sorted through the findings and shared them with our instructional team. Detailed written memos of the findings were sent to all members of the instructional team, and these findings were shared at faculty, CPM, weekly building team, and weekly SLC coordinators meetings.

After many discussions with members of the instructional team, the administrative team—which included two assistant principals, the SCL facilitator, the language arts and the math coach, the technology coordinator, two guidance counselors, the school social worker, and a principal—decided that we would design a professional learning program that would address our instructional needs.

We decided that the instructional model had to contain instructional strategies that enabled teachers to teach students of varying abilities and learning styles, inspire students to engage in critical thinking, and take responsibility for their own learning. Differentiated instruction, Socratic method, learning stations, and cooperative learning groups method were the components of our professional learning model. As time passed, we referred to these instructional strategies as reform strategies.

After many discussions, group meetings, individual meetings, and conversations with experts from higher education, we had evidence that the majority of our staff embraced our professional learning model; and we prepared to move forward. The administrative team and the instructional staff believed that we had enough talented teachers on staff at OMS to provide some of the required professional learning. Other professional development would be provided by Rutgers University, Seton Hall, and other individual providers.

We developed workshops for professional learning, which our master teachers facilitated: the language arts coach and special education teacher facilitated a workshop on differentiated instruction, a language arts teacher and two science teachers facilitated a workshop on learning stations, the SLC facilitated cooperative learning groups, and the principal facilitated a workshop on the Socratic method. Workshops for differentiated instruction, learning stations, and cooperative learning groups were scheduled during faculty meetings. The Socratic method was scheduled during the CPMs of each SLC. The staff received in-service credit for attending these workshops, which could be used toward earning advance degrees.

Learning is a treasure that will follow its owner everywhere.

—John Ciardi

Professional Learning on Differentiated Instruction

The professional learning on differentiated instruction offered the staff specific strategies for addressing the different learning styles of their students. The facilitator led a discussion that related to the research of Howard Gardner's work on multiple intelligences. As she discussed Gardner's list of the seven intelligences, some of our teachers began to match their students' learning patterns with the descriptors that were presented. We discussed instructional activities that could offer students greater insight into their learning style. The teachers gained insight into the importance of taking measures to understand the individual learning needs of their students and that they were pleased to receive specific strategies that they could use to adjust their classroom instruction accordingly.

This workshop was particularly important for teachers who taught inclusion classes. Inclusion teachers were urged to develop their lesson plans together and assume equal responsibility for teaching all students by incorporating accommodations for the different learning styles of their special education and regular education students. They began a dialogue, which resulted in them realizing that there were many approaches for teaching their students that they had overlooked. Based upon the strengths of the two teachers' talent, sometimes they needed to follow a model of whole group instruction and other times the students needed to be grouped into cooperative learning groups; other times they needed a conferencing model to offer individual assistance or small-group discussion to students. The teachers were shown DVDs that presented examples of classroom instruction, where students were taught to accommodate for the disabilities of their classmates. These DVDs were tapes of teachers' classrooms within the district. The teachers began to understand that the goal was for the instruction to appear seamless, and this could not happen unless the teachers developed their lesson plans together.

It's a miracle that curiosity survives formal education.

—Albert Einstein

Professional Learning
on Learning Stations

The professional learning on learning stations involved a science lab on the theory of plate tectonics. The students were divided into four cooperative learning groups (CLG). Each CLG was required to rotate and complete the instructional activities at each of the four science lab stations. The teachers observing this DVD were intrigued by the level of rigor and the intellectual endeavor involved at each learning station as the students completed the following tasks: at the earthquake learning station, the students graphed the seismic movement of earthquakes using data from the United States Geological Survey (USGS); at the volcanic learning station, students made models to track the flow of magma to show how the Hawaiian Islands were formed; at the midocean ridges learning station, the students viewed a DVD from the Woods Hole Oceanographic Institution of volcanic geysers and answered questions about the shifting of the Mid-Atlantic plates between Europe and North America continents; and at the fourth earth science learning station, students used ice models to demonstrate the effect of "extreme pressures" upon the movement of the Earth's plates.

After viewing the DVD, the staff divided themselves into their SLCs and functioned as CLGs. Each CLG was given a specific set of questions to respond to. A presenter from each CLG reported their group's findings to the faculty.

Some of the insights that were shared included they had a clearer understanding of how to: (1) design instruction using learning stations model, (2) facilitate CLGM in their classrooms as result of their participation in this workshop, (3) develop rigorous tasks when using the CLGM, (4) effectively employ two instructional practices so that they work in concert with one another, and (5) make instructional tasks that are employed in the CLGM more relevant. One staff member's comment was "students behaved like young scientists."

A problem is a chance for you to do your best.

—Duke Ellington

Professional Learning of the Cooperative Learning Group Model

The Professional Learning workshop was facilitated by the SLC facilitator. The CLGs were organized according to the subjects that the teachers taught. Each CLG was given test data on their students and their task was, based on the test data that was given to them, to design a measurable instructional strategy to improve academic achievement. Each CLG was given descriptions of the roles involved in the CLGM. Their job was to read these descriptors and make a decision on who would serve in the capacity of each role: team leader, team recorder, timekeeper, and team presenter. The CLGs were given ten minutes of uninterrupted time to complete their task. The facilitator developed a rubric scoring system and gave the results to each CLG after each presentation was completed.

The facilitator introduced the objective clearly and precisely. The behavior of the teachers paralleled the behavior of a typical class of students. Some CLGs worked more effectively than others and quickly decided on the roles that each would assume. The administrators served as facilitators. The administrators were careful to follow the guidelines of the CLGM. When we visited our assigned CLG, we only spoke to the team leader. If we had questions regarding the pace that a particular CLG was working at, we addressed the team leader and not the participant who asked the question. If a participant other than the team leader asked a question, we redirected the question to the team leader. We wanted each CLG to understand that the purpose of a CLG is to solve problems collaboratively and to take responsibility for their learning.

This instructional activity underscored how it could be utilized to raise academic achievement on state assessments. The teachers stated that they gained insight into (1)understanding the components of the CLGM, (2)designing rigorous tasks and understanding the importance of the roles involved in the CLGM, (3) developing strategies at the beginning of the assignment that were coordinated with the timekeeper so that they could remain on task and meet the responsibilities associated with their roles, and (4)understanding the importance of the facilitator honoring each CLG by allowing them to work without interruptions.

This activity successfully demonstrated the strengths gained from using the CLGM. Prior to this demonstration, the staff had a habit of placing students in groups and assuming that they were employing the CLGM.

Tell me and I'll forget, show me and I may remember,
involve me and I'll understand.

—Chinese Proverb

Professional Learning
on the Socratic Method

The principal facilitated the workshop for professional learning on the Socratic method. Five workshops were scheduled during the common planning periods for each SLC. Each team met in the same quiet location. Immediately, after settling in, an audio recording of Robert Kennedy's speech on the assassination of Dr. Martin Luther King Jr. was introduced, and copies of this speech were distributed to each participant.

After listening to this speech, the principal posed as Socrates and asked a series of Socratic questions designed to inspire the participants to heighten their critical thinking skills, understand the importance of the use of the Socratic method and Socratic questions, become familiar with the six types of Socratic questions, and enable the participants to design applications for use of this instructional strategy.

To illustrate to the teachers the importance of providing evidence for each response that was elicited, the facilitator professed complete ignorance of all matters associated with the Socratic method. The questions utilized in this activity were similar to those found on the NJ ASK and included both open-ended and inference questions.

The teachers gained insight into the definition of critical thinking; the use of the Socratic method as a tool to inspire critical thinking; the difference between facts, assumptions, opinions, deductive reasoning, and judgments; the skill of making inferences; the development of open-ended questions; and the application of this instructional strategy for classroom activities.

The teachers were impressed with the way this workshop quickly developed into a meaningful discussion that could be used when designing lesson plans. At times, they engaged in heated debates that caused them to lose themselves as they expressed their positions. In each case, they stated that they understood this instructional activity aided in the development of critical thinking skills.

An education isn't how much you have committed to memory, or even how much you know. It's being able to differentiate between what you do know and what you don't know.

—Anatole France

Rigor

Once the instructional team began to have conversations about improving student learning, discussions around classroom rigor began to evolve. The administrative team reflected on the occasion when a small team of consultants visited OMS for the specific purpose of developing a reform strategy to increase the level of classroom rigor. This team wanted to begin their work with those teachers that were considered the better teachers. These were the teachers that always submitted good lesson plans that were aligned to the NJCCCS, had high level of student engagement, were highly motivated, and taught students who believed that they were good teachers. Whenever we visited the classrooms of these teachers, there always seemed to be a high level of student and teacher satisfaction, and they always achieved the instructional objectives, which were clearly presented to their students. We assumed that the team of consultants would observe a high level of rigor when we visited these classes.

This team of consultants went into a language arts class of one of these teachers, which was organized around four learning stations devoted to poetry; and we noted that at each learning station, the students understood the expectations and were working independently. After the team observed the instructional activities at each station, we discussed our findings. We concluded that none of the four learning stations offered the students sophisticated reflective learning experiences. The competencies learned at each learning station did not afford the students an appropriate challenge. The tasks did not require students to engage in analysis, distinguish facts from opinions, or listen with a critical mind. Instead, they responded to tasks that required objective reflections. At one learning station, the students were required to draw pictures of poetic literary terms that included alliteration, hyperbole, metaphor, onomatopoeia, simile, and personification. The team of consultants concluded that a more rigorous assignment would have been to include noted poems and poets, which would have inspired higher order of thinking.

This experience made it clear to the administrative team that the OMS, did not meet the standard of the appropriate level of rigor in our classrooms.

As I reflect on the issue of classroom rigor, I agree with Wagner (2006) that there was no common agreement on what rigor is. In 2002, he introduced the new three

Rs: rigor, relevance, and respectful relationships. He concluded that relevance and respectful relationships are essential elements in motivating students to want to achieve rigor. Although the instructional team at OMS did not review Wagner's work at the time we were engaged in our study on rigor, in retrospect, it's worthwhile to compare his efforts to those that were initiated at OMS.

Wagner was challenged by a group of principals from Kona, Hawaii, to think about what his new three Rs actually looked like in the classroom. They explored basic questions about rigor. "What are teachers doing in a rigorous classroom, and what does rigorous work look like at different grade levels?" It did not take long before they realized how difficult their task was. After two days, the principals realized that rigor had less to do with how demanding the material that the teacher covers is and more to do with what competencies the students master as a result of the instruction that is taught. They realized that the real power of their work came from their having to think through for themselves what rigor is instead of being told.

Similarly, the instructional team at OMS worked through the practical meaning of rigor for our purposes. After extended communication, we agreed that we had to have a definitive way of defining the challenging tasks associated with rigor; and we agreed on proficient and advanced proficient, meaning rigor had to result in proficient or advanced-proficient outcomes. This was a good beginning for the work that followed.

Seven student questions related to rigor emerged from Wagner's work:

1. What is the purpose of the lesson?
2. Why is it important to learn?
3. In what ways are the students challenged to think as a result of the instruction?
4. How can the student apply, assess, or communicate what they have learned?
5. How will the students know how good their work is, and how can they improve upon it?
6. When engaged in the instructional activity, do the students feel respected by other students in the classroom?
7. When engaged in the instructional activity, do the students feel respected by their teacher?

Wagner's study led him to the use of these seven questions repeatedly. Similarly, the learning that resulted from the professional learning at OMS was embraced by staff throughout the district.

Successful executives and professionals know that the
price of excellence is careful preparation.

The Lesson Plan

The OMS administrative team agreed one approach of assuring quality instruction for all students attending OMS was to require our teachers' lesson plans be aligned with the New Jersey Core Curriculum Content Standards (NJCCCS) and that these lesson plans include instructional strategies that inspire students to become critical thinkers and independent learners. The instructional staff was encouraged to employ any instructional strategy that would enable them to attain this goal, and that included the instructional strategies of our reform model: Socratic questioning, differentiated instruction, accountable talk, formative assessment, learning stations, and cooperative learning groups model. OMS was in the early stages of school reform; well-developed lesson plans were viewed as road maps, that would lead to good instruction.

The New Jersey state requirement of proper alignment for all required courses was an important measure for school reform. All major courses at OMS were properly aligned. Language arts, math, science, social studies, foreign language, art, music, and physical education were aligned with the NJCCCS. The NJCCCS in turn were aligned with the national standards. The administrative team knew that a good monitoring system would reflect this alignment, and this would have a powerful impact upon instruction at OMS. The administrative team set up a monitoring protocol by departments. Each of the three administrators was responsible for reviewing one third of the teaching staff's instructional lesson plans biweekly. Accountability was the key component involved in this important monitoring procedure. We checked to see if their lesson plans were aligned with NJCCCS, if they followed the OMS scope and sequences that had been developed for each of the course offered, and if the teachers followed the established district lesson plan format. Most importantly, we expected to see these elements in the instruction that they taught when we visited their classrooms.

Initially, many teachers did not understand the importance of well-developed instructional lesson plans. Some teachers submitted instructional lesson plans that reflected little care or concern. While many instructional lesson plans appeared to be credible because they had all the components of our established lesson plan format and they were in the proper sequence, they were not credible. Further examination reflected that lesson plans were copied from the many available resources that were available and groups of teachers had identical lesson plans. More disturbing was that in most of these cases, when the administrative team visited their classrooms, the content and the implementation strategies did not match the instructional lesson plans that had been submitted.

The OMS administrative team quickly learned how to use the teachers' lesson plans and classroom visits as talking points for improving instruction at OMS.

It was routine for OMS administrative team to invest six to seven hours on the review of our teachers' instructional lesson plans. These plans were always returned with comments that reflected that we had carefully read them and we were monitoring to see if their lesson plans were aligned with the NJCCCS and the scope and sequence of the given course, included the outlined instructional strategies, and contained instructional methods that inspired students to become critical thinkers and independent learners. The administrative team employed the Socratic method to bring about some of the instructional changes that we wanted. Examples of the questions that we included as part of the lesson plan feedback form were the following:

1. Can you include the specific standard that is reflective of this lesson objective?
2. What portion of your instructional lesson are you employing whole group instruction?
3. Is there a more appropriate instructional strategy that could result in greater student-directed learning?
4. Are you employing accountable talk during whole-group instruction?
5. How often are you employing the CLGM?
6. What measure of formative assessment are you employing to determine if your students understand the objectives that are being taught?
7. Have you considered using podcasting as part of the CLGM?
8. Sometimes we suggested websites to be included as part of the instructional lesson.
9. We also wrote comments such as "I see that you are implementing learning stations on Tuesday. Have you had success with this instructional strategy before? I will drop by to observe and to support your efforts." The administrator would then arrange their schedule so that he/she set time aside to visit and have a follow-up discussion with that teacher.
10. Would it help if you employed more Socratic questions during the "Do Now?" portion of your instructional lesson?

Sometimes the administrative team would simply include a simple comment—"This lesson plan is well developed and comprehensive. I'd like to stop by on a given date to see this particular instructional strategy." Our objective was to let our teachers know that the administrative team and other staff members were available to support their professional growth. The reaction from the staff was impressive. They could be found at their mailboxes, reading the lesson plan feedback form. The feedback form was not used as a checklist; it was used as an instructional tool. As time passed, the level of trust between the administrative team and the teachers increased, and the quality of lesson plans improved.

OMS teachers began to realize that there was a high correlation between the efforts that they put into the preparation of their instructional lessons and quality that resulted. Often, the effective teachers remained in the building long after working hours. Sometimes, these same teachers request extensions beyond the due date because they needed more time to gain insight to implement a new instructional strategy. Their request was always granted, and their instructional plans always reflected that the time was well spent. When the administrators visited their classrooms, we found a high level of student participation, great rapport between the teacher and their students, and an appropriate level of rigor associated with each of the instructional activities that were employed. There was always a sense of comfort and ease with their instruction because they had taken all the necessary measures to offer their students the best possible opportunities for learning. These teachers were impressed with their growth and cared about their profession and our school and never hesitated to volunteer to facilitate workshops at faculty meetings. Interestingly enough, the more the administrative team spoke about instructional advances, the larger this group became.

The effective teachers understood that they had to take prerequisites into account. They had a good understanding of their students' state of readiness. They included the skills that students needed to have mastered prior to the date that the lesson was to be taught. They knew if they wanted 100 percent of their students to successfully understand the objectives outlined in their instructional lesson plans, they had to teach prerequisite skills. Their instructional lesson plans also included the concepts that the students needed to know in advance of the instruction that they planned to present. This data was not only important for its current use but was also useful for their future professional efforts. They developed a library of instructional lesson plans and exchanged them with other teachers within their department and within their SLC and, in many instances, made them available for any teacher in the school who could benefit from them. These instructional lesson plans involved numerous hours of tedious professional effort, and the consensus was, they should be shared. With the rapid change in technology and the constant changes in the medical, social, and political landscapes, a new set of eyes often resulted in the enhancement of the original instructional lesson plans. Teachers who used plans from the library understood that would have to adjust them to their teaching style and to the instructional relevancy of their students.

The OMS lesson plan format included all the standard elements: NJCCCS, lesson objectives, materials, procedure, homework, evaluation, websites/technology, and special projects/notes/differentiation. The teachers were trained to write the objectives by stating what they expected their students to learn (i.e., students will be able to . . .). The teachers were encouraged to begin with the end in mind, meaning a concise statement of the goal that was to be achieved by the end of the instructional block. Some teachers who understood the importance of writing an objective statement therefore put in a significant amount of time to explain the overall lesson and included specific steps and terminology so that it could be easily understood and duplicated. When writing the objective statement, effective teachers included the conditions that were needed to accomplish the objectives. Another important component of the objective statement was the evidence that was presented to demonstrate that students attained the skills or knowledge that were taught. Teachers who took the task of writing well-developed instructional lesson plans seriously expressed that students' outcomes improved exponentially as they increased the amount of time that they devoted to gaining clarity of the objectives presented in their instructional lesson plans.

The daily objectives were always developed with the objectives of the broader unit in mind. Our teachers were required to include not only what students will accomplish but also the percentage of students in their class that will be able to achieve the objectives. While the administrative team encouraged the teachers to be honest, we were taken aback by the number of teachers who did not expect 100 percent of their students to understand the objectives that they planned to teach. Differentiated instruction was used to address this concern. While it was painful to acknowledge this, we were pleased that the teachers trusted us enough to present this matter honestly. Effective teachers would state that they expected 85 percent of their students to understand the objectives. Other teachers presented percentages were as low as 70 percent. The instructional lesson plan contained valuable information, and we learned when we used this information properly, it was an effective barometer of the measure of learning that was occurring at OMS. This also is a reflection of the challenges that confront classroom teachers. Teachers often shared the impact that extenuating circumstances had upon delivery of instruction, including poverty—the hardships that students faced that they had no control over or problems resulting from transient students, students reading below grade level, students entering or leaving classrooms at inopportune times, and/or disturbances outside the school that filtered into classrooms. Teachers reported that when students faced these kinds of issues, it was extremely difficult to get them to focus on instruction. Teachers also had to use their intellect to prevent any problem from spiraling out of control. There is no question that it is more challenging to teach in a community that is confronted by economic and social challenges than one that is not. However, having said that, the students must be afforded high quality education regardless of where they live.

The most important consideration made relating to the selection of materials was—it had to be—relevant to the objectives, leading to high student retention, and enhancing student learning.

The administrative team encouraged teachers to employ the problem-solving-style lesson plans for a variety of reasons: test data reflected limited skills and knowledge were attained by our students when teachers relied heavily on lecture style of teaching. On the other hand, test data and our day-to-day observations reflected that our students improved in a number of areas of instructional outcomes when our teachers employed a problem-solving style of teaching. Some of the factors that were noted included a higher level of student engagement, improvement of their critical thinking skills, an increase in the number of students who were inspired and expressed a desire to learn, an improvement in the learning environment, and an improvement in academic achievement. Therefore, for these reasons, this style of teaching was encouraged.

Each of our five small learning communities was responsible for the development of one interdisciplinary unit per quarter. This requirement advanced the quality of instruction throughout our school. It entailed the core subject teachers of each SLC creating interdisciplinary instructional lessons. A portion of the common planning time was devoted to this initiative. These thematic interdisciplinary units always resulted in impressive projects that were displayed throughout our building. The instructional staff reported that these instructional experiences heightened student motivation of nearly every student, and students benefited from the connections that they were able to make as they traveled from one core subject to the next. Equally as important, it inspired many of our students to become independent learners and initiate academic projects above and beyond the required assignments.

In every instance when interdisciplinary thematic units were properly planned, the results were similar to those described in a Michigan School District, which created integrated plans for thematic units based on the ideas of Howard Gardner's multiple intelligences, where they included "sustained enthusiasm" from staff, parents, and students; increased attendance rates; and improvement in standardized test scores, "especially from students with the poorest test results" (Bolak, Bialach, and Duhnphy, 2005).

The professional development for the design and implementation of the interdisciplinary thematic units began one year before OMS implemented the SLCM. The professional learning that resulted from this experience prepared our school facilitator and our SLC coordinators to undertake the rigors involved in this challenging initiative. These workshops afforded them the opportunity to discuss and investigate current research in this area of planning and implementing interdisciplinary thematic units. They became familiar with techniques that could be used by staff and students for the selection of themes that they could consider for units of study and specific implementation procedures. They discussed factors that resulted in an increase in parental involvement. As a result of these well-designed workshops, our school facilitator and SLC coordinators were able to work collaboratively and effectively on the design and implementation of the OMS requirement of quarterly interdisciplinary thematic units. The OMS parents and students reaped several significant benefits from this requirement, including greater opportunities for engagement of students in in-depth research on a topic of interest and relevancy, increased opportunities for teachers to provide differentiated instruction for students who required individualized attention and for gifted and talented students enabling them to express individual talent, students' understanding of the importance of working as collaborative teams, increased parent involvement in their child's school assignments, improvement of the school climate, and improvement of the level of job satisfaction for staff members. The administrative team used every available forum to highlight this impressive work, including advertisements and announcements on district websites and at PTA meetings and mandatory meetings with parents (i.e., back-to-school night). When visitors toured our school, they were given a detailed briefing of the interdisciplinary projects.

The lesson plans designed for the interdisciplinary thematic units met the established instructional lesson plan requirements. All thematic units had to meet the NJCCCS for language arts, math, science, and social studies. This initiative resulted in many successful thematic units. The thematic units of Visual Arts SLC included "The History of Orange," "Exploring Our World," "Orange Goes Green," "Heroes," "Out of This World," "Immigration," and "Crime Scene Investigation." The thematic units of Law and Order SLC included "Liberty under Law," "Empowering Youth," "Assuring Democracy," "Elis Island," "Constitution Day," "Your Vote Is Your Voice," "The Rule of the Law," and "Election 2008." Some of the thematic units of Health Sciences SLC were "Health Wellness," "Aquatic Life," "The Biology and the Politics of Stem Cell Research," "Election '08," "Global Warming," "Distance Learning," "Universal Health Care Issues," "The Changes We Need for the 21st Century," "H1N1 Virus and You," and "Forensic Science in Motion." Some of the thematic units of Technology-Math SLC included "The Character Threads of Well-known People," "Wellness Matters," "Inventors," "Inventions, Discoveries, and Life Experiences," and "Aquatic Animals." The thematic units of Prodigy Hall SLC included "Performance Hall, We Will Be Stars," "Who Am I, Everybody Counts," "The Last Lecture," "Michael Jackson," "Service Learning," and "Earthquakes."

There were visual signs of these thematic units throughout the OMS. Our school nurse collaborated with the Health Sciences SLC, and consequently, the entire school district became involved in the national health and wellness initiative. This meant the entire school district reverted to only serving and selling healthy foods. The Health Sciences SLC engaged in extensive exploration of healthy ways of eating and exercising. A group of students who wanted to address issues relating to childhood obesity evolved; this group was completely voluntary and nonjudgmental.

Other activities and events that resulted from the thematic units included "Black History Program," which was created and produced by Prodigy Hall, the creation of a garden in the school's courtyard by Visual Arts SLC, and an extensive study of the US Constitution by the Law and Order SLC, which included the creation of a guest speaker's bureau and annual participation in Law Day competitive competition at a city government office in Newark, New Jersey; talented student orators evolved from Technology-Math SLC.

Orange Middle School Plan Book

Teacher:	Week of:	Periods: 1 & 4
Subject/Grade: Language Arts/8	Room:	Unit:
Text:		

Monday	**Tuesday**	**Wednesday**	**Thursday**	**Friday**
Topics:	Topics:	Topics:	Topics:	Topics:
Objectives: ___ % of students will be able to (insert HOTS verb) as a result of (insert instructional modality) with ___% proficiency or better	Objectives: ___ % of students will be able to as a result of teacher modeling and student practice with ___% proficiency or better	Objectives: ___ % of students will be able to (insert HOTS verb) as a result of (insert instructional modality) with ___% proficiency or better	Objectives: ___ % of students will be able to (insert HOTS verb) as a result of (insert instructional modality) with ___% proficiency or better	Objectives: ___ % of students will be able to (insert HOTS verb) as a result of (insert instructional modality) with ___% proficiency or better
Materials:	Materials:	Materials:	Materials:	Materials:
Procedures:	Procedures:	Procedures:	Procedures:	Procedures:
Homework:	Homework:	Homework:	Homework:	Homework:
Evaluation:	Evaluation:	Evaluation:	Evaluation:	Evaluation:
Websites/ Technology:	Websites/ Technology:	Websites/ Technology:	Websites/ Technology:	Websites/ Technology:
NJCCCS:	NJCCCS:	NJCCCS:	NJCCCS:	NJCCCS:
Special Projects/Notes/ Differentiation:				

Recently, OMS adopted the Orange Middle School Understanding by Design (UbD) lesson plan format. It is based upon the research of Grant Wiggins and Jay McTighe. Understanding by Design (UbD) is the practice of looking at the outcomes in order to design curriculum units, performance assessments, and classroom instruction.

UbD is a framework for improving student achievement and is based upon the assumption that the teacher is the chief architect or designer of student learning. It works within the standards-driven curriculum to help teachers clarify learning goals, devise revealing assessments of student learning, and craft effective and engaging learning activities. The goal is for the students to attain a deep understanding of what is being taught. It was developed by nationally recognized educators Grant Wiggins and Jay McTighe and published by the Association for Supervision and Curriculum Development (ASCD).

In practice, Understanding by Design offers a three-stage "backward planning" curriculum design process anchored by unit design template; a set of design standards with attendant rubrics; and a comprehensive training package to help teachers design, edit critique, peer-review, share, and improve their lesson and assessments (Wiggins and McTighe, 1998).

Learning is taught with the expectation that students will be able to explain, have perspective, apply, interpret, empathize, and have self-knowledge about the given classroom topic. Implementation of this model was not a major philosophical shift. Similar to the OMS instructional lesson plan format, UbD, which is often referred to as the backward design, starts with classroom outcomes and then plans the curriculum, choosing instructional activities and materials that help determine student ability and that which will result in learning.

Teaching for understanding is the central focus of UbD and was the critical component that inspired OMS to embrace it as an instructional tool. Through professional development, a significant number of the OMS teachers are gaining an appreciation that teaching for understanding must be evident in all aspects of their lesson, including the learning environment and attitudes of the teacher and the student. Equally important, teachers learned the value of having a coherent curriculum, developing big ideas and essential questions and the distinction between the two, performance requirements, and the evaluative criteria. OMS teachers understood the importance of presenting these concepts to their students at the beginning of the instructional block.

Dr. Judith Kronin

Orange Middle School

Understanding by Design Template

Teacher_____ **Grade**_____
Date_____ **Subject**_____

Stage 1—Desired Results	
Established Goals:	
Understandings: Students will understand that . . .	**Essential Questions:**
Students will know . . .	Students will be able to . . .

Stage 2—Assessment Evidence	
Performance Tasks:	**Other Evidence:**
Self-assessments	**Other Evidence, Summarized**
Stage 3—Learning Plan	
Learning Activities:	

The whole purpose of education is to turn mirrors into windows.

—Sidney J. Harris

CHAPTER THREE

Orange Middle School Is Honored

In the spring of '08, I was entering a restaurant in Greenwich Village, New York, New York, when I received a phone call from the Title 1 director of our district informing me that Orange Middle School was the recipient of an award in the amount of $100,000 from the Mid-Atlantic Compliance Center, the federal overseers of No Child Left Behind funding and implementation for Washington DC, Delaware, Maryland, Virginia, New Jersey, and Pennsylvania, for being one of several schools that established effective practices that resulted in significant gains in student achievement. Although this accolade was totally unexpected, it confirmed that it was time for the Orange Middle School staff to be recognized for their professional efforts. In lieu of the first June faculty meeting, the building administrative team organized a celebration honoring all OMS instructional team. They were served dinner from the best Italian restaurant in town and presented with certificates. The OMS instructional team had carefully navigated a path that led to quality instruction. We had articulated a quality instructional program that was capable of expanding our knowledge base and serving as a reference point for future professional development and learning.

The Mid-Atlantic Compliance Center Team requested a four-hour visit to become acquainted with the instructional practices that the OMS instructional staff had used to attain the significant gain in student achievement.

As we prepared for this important meeting, we began with a discussion of how pleased we were by the accolade. We had not expected to be acknowledged for significant improvement in student achievement. Nonetheless, we were ecstatic that our state assessment scores reflected significant growth, causing OMS to be acknowledged by the prestigious Mid-Atlantic Compliance Center. The entire instructional team believed our students and our school could benefit from this visit.

The agenda for this meeting between Orange School District and the Mid-Atlantic Compliance Team was developed. It included introductions, the transition from a traditional middle school model to the small learning communities model, the benefits that resulted from fully embracing the SLCM, the development and use of the reform strategies, and a question-and-answer session. Those in attendance included the assistant superintendent for curriculum and instruction, director of special services, OMS guidance staff, SLC facilitator, assistant principals, SLC coordinators, academic coaches, technology coordinator, and union representatives.

The visit affirmed that the instructional tasks that we had engaged in over the past two and a half years were valid for improving classroom instruction. It had not been easy, but our persistence and perseverance had paid off. The majority of the members in each small learning community were effectively using our instructional model for the delivery of instruction.

The acknowledgement by the visiting team heightened the level of professionalism throughout the building. Staff morale and teacher confidence rose. As we moved forward, we realized that the instructional staff was assuming greater responsibility for improving classroom instruction. The instructional staff from each SLC felt comfortable using the system that was in place to address the day-to-day operational concerns. The visiting team was very impressed with the display of the interdisciplinary projects. This reaction motivated the teachers and the students and resulted in an increase in the number and the quality of interdisciplinary projects. We also noticed that the visit stimulated creative juices to flow in other areas as well. Conversations involving the use of technology were among the important topics that were discussed after the visit, and as an administrative team, we were pleased. We understood that technology was a wise investment and that it was capable of changing the way students learn. It opened new doors and helped students engage in their learning experiences as suggested by Brumfield (2005).

Education is simply the soul of a society as it
passes from one generation to another.

—Cornelius Vanderbilt

Interim Superintendent of Orange Public Schools

At the August 18, 2008, special session of the Orange Board of Education meeting, I became the interim superintendent of Orange Public Schools, replacing the outgoing superintendent. During my introduction to the community, the board president cited some of the achievements accomplished at OMS. The instructional team was credited with the revision of the school dress policy and bringing stability to Orange Middle School. A significant number of stakeholders believed that the same practices that turned Orange Middle School around could improve the quality of instruction throughout the entire district. That evening the stakeholders emphasized, "Together we can make Orange School District a world-class learning center." We were committed to increasing the level of achievement for all students attending our schools. Initially, our focus included the design and implementation of a quarterly benchmark assessment for grades K–12, measures which would raise the level of rigor in the curriculum and inspire students to take responsibility for their learning.

Rather than having my cabinet concern itself with the enormity of the situation, I started the process by introducing myself to central office staff, the principals, and staff in each building. My goal was to simply let them know that the plan was to work collaboratively with them and all members of the community. Close relationships with my secretary, Board of Education members, and principals began to evolve. Learning the hectic schedule of a superintendent was the first task that was tackled. Secondly, I began meeting regularly with a mentor who was an experienced superintendent from another school district. The latter was a critical step in the early stages as superintendent. Understanding the roles and responsibilities of each of my cabinet members and being able to work well with all board members was next item of responsibility. Once I understood the enormity of the position, I began working with members of my cabinet to develop a plan for improving instruction in each of our eleven schools and the prekindergarten program.

To make sure that every school within the district was teaching and assessing the same curriculum, we created a committee, which included representatives from each school, every grade, and every subject, to develop the K–12 quarterly benchmark assessment tool. The purpose was to assure that every subject taught in grades K–12 were aligned with the standards, included skills and resources, and was assessed on the fifth and tenth weeks of each of the quarter. This resource tool guaranteed uniformity for all courses that were taught, increased the likelihood of mastery of required skills, identified the skills that were taught, and created uniform assessments for all subjects. This data is stored electronically and can be periodically updated. A committee of seventy instructional staff members completed the task over a four-month period. The value of the quarterly benchmark assessment cannot be overstated.

Good teaching is one-fourth preparation and three-fourths theatre.

—Gail Godwin

District Walk-throughs

The instructional staff at Orange Middle School was always prepared to share their professional learning skills with colleagues throughout the district. A twelve-member OMS team who attended the August 2008 Rutgers Institute for Improving Student Achievement (RIISA) at Rutgers University presented a workshop to all Orange District principals and supervisors on accountable talk, new intelligence, Socratic method, learning stations, cooperative learning group model, and formative assessment. It proved to be a valuable professional development program, and it afforded district office staff, principals, and supervisors an opportunity to become familiar with the reform strategies. It also enabled the district an opportunity to begin to converse as a community of learners. The principals followed up this experience by designing similar workshops for the staff at each of their schools. As the incoming superintendent, I benefited from each of these professional development initiatives. Collectively, they proved to be invaluable. This was an important first for communicating my vision for improving classroom instruction to all members of the instructional team within the district.

I recognized that there were pockets of effective instruction taking place at each of our schools in Orange; therefore, I directed district members of the curriculum and instruction team to design a district walk-through initiative to support and monitor classroom instruction throughout the district. The plan included quarterly visits to two classrooms in each of our schools to observe and support classroom instruction. These informal visits were designed to give principals and teachers immediate feedback on the observation. Initially, the walk-through team was made up of the interim superintendent, assistant superintendent for curriculum and instruction, a principal, a supervisor, or a coach. The principal selected two classes, which were observed for fifteen minutes.

We decided to start the walk-through initiative by encouraging all instructional staff to gain an understanding of the cooperative learning group model (CLGM). All staff received a memo with the definitions of the reform strategies. This was followed up with meetings and discussions on cooperative learning group model (CLGM). The scheduled principal meetings focused on CLGM, and conversations and discussions on this topic were encouraged. On the building level, supervisors and coaches assisted teachers by designing CLGM workshops and by coaching them in the classroom. Ms.

Frazier, the assistant superintendent for curriculum and instruction, created a district walk-through schedule for visits to all our schools, and thus, the district walk-throughs began.

We created a district walk-through form, which included all the reform strategies. Although initially, our concentration was on the CLGM, the members of the walk-through team were requested to observe two specific reform strategies each. The discussion that followed each walk-through began with positive comments about the instruction that was observed. One member of the team asked each member and the teacher to share one item or aspect of the instructional lesson that they felt was effective. The second and the final question was to share one item that they should be improved. The completed walk-through form was given to the teacher shortly after the visit. The walk-through, which was not part of the formal evaluation process, did not require a teacher's signature.

The walk-throughs were an immediate success. Teachers from each of our schools often expressed that these visits gave them a sense that their professional efforts were being acknowledged. They liked the opportunity that it afforded them of being able to share their instructional concerns and issues with members of the administrative team. They viewed the walk-through as an additional resource and associated the visit with being singled out for special acknowledgment. Further, the teachers involved expressed that as a result of the walk-throughs, they believed that the superintendent had a greater appreciation of the day-to-day challenges that they encountered in the classroom. We believed that part of the success of the district walk-throughs were the open lines of communication. A minor but significant point associated with that district walk-through schedule was the availability to everyone throughout the district.

Much was learned from this practice. The instructional staff gained a more in-depth understanding of the meaning and use of each reform strategy. The walk-through team developed a clearer understanding of the meaning of effective instruction, and we began to envision effective instruction in each of our schools. With regard to the implementation of the reform strategies, it revealed that some schools were ahead of others. These walk-throughs enabled members of the cabinet, principals, supervisors, and coaches to recognize learning deficiencies and to design specific workshops to address these learning deficiencies. It also enabled administrators to become acquainted with the "master teachers" throughout the district, meaning those teachers who had mastered the art of teaching and consistently created and utilized effective instructional strategies.

Master teachers became instrumental components for moving the reform movement forward. After the walk-throughs, a cadre of master teachers was identified. This enabled administrators to match master teachers with teachers who desired and needed to master specific instructional strategies. Teacher visitation schedules were then established for visitations within the school and for visitations from other schools.

Coupled with this, we recognized the benefit of creating DVDs of each reform strategy—CLGM, accountable talk, Socratic questions, formative assessment, differentiated instruction, and learning stations were realized. We asked our master teachers for their assistance, and they obliged. Under the direction of our technology coordinator, our technology students assisted in creating and duplicating DVDs for each reform strategy. These DVDs became powerful instructional tools at meetings and workshops. Individual teachers used them to gain clarity about particular reform strategies. Building coaches used them at workshops, and in a relatively short amount of time, they became experts of particular reform strategies and, consequently, facilitated a greater number of instructional workshops.

District Walk-through Visitation Form

TEACHER:				
SUBJECT/GRADE:				
ROOM #:				
DATE:				
I. STANDARDS EVIDENT	II. STUDENT ENGAGEMENT	III. WORD WALL	IV. INSTRUCTIONAL STATEGY	V. COMMUNICATION & CRITICAL THINKING

YES	HIGH	Lesson Objective	Portfolios	Socratic Questions
NO	MEDIUM	NJCCCS Notebooks	LOW	Learning Centers

Bulletin Boards
Student's Understanding Cooperative Learning Group
Class Rules of Instruction   Differentiated Instruction
Technology Evidence of Independent Learning
Word Wall Student Work

COMMENTS:
ADMINISTRATOR:

The school is the last expenditure upon which
America should be willing to economize.

—Franklin D. Roosevelt

The Education Instructional Coaching Model (EICM)

As the scheduled district walk-throughs continued, the instructional staff began to appreciate the implications of our efforts, and we began to envision a real possibility of developing effective schools, where all students had access to quality instruction. We understood the importance of the reform strategies that were being utilized throughout the district. They had been the basis for the success that resulted in an increase in student achievement at Orange Middle School, and we believed that they could also be effective in raising the level of student achievement throughout the district. Coupled with this, there was agreement that the district walk-through initiative was an effective tool for monitoring classroom instruction. As time passed, it became clear that these two components were having a powerful impact on our plan for school reform, and members of our instructional team perceived these two components as the foundation for an effective coaching model. With the understanding that we needed an educational model that could be utilized by all teachers in grades K–12, we continued to persist and the Education Instructional Coaching Model (EICM) evolved from these two components: the reform strategies and the district walk-through initiative.

Initially, we started with the Orange walk-through team visiting classrooms throughout the district for the purpose of promoting meaningful classroom practices that would improve classroom instruction and ultimately it was beginning to result in the creation high-performing schools. We recognized that school improvement is a continuous team effort that requires the commitment of all stakeholders. Further, we understood if we expected to be successful, we had to support the efforts of our instructional staff. Although it was not articulated in retrospect, our goal was for EICM to be a model that could be used in any school district that is interested in raising academic achievement by using an inquiry-based or problem-solving approach.

Membership into the EICM team was open to all members of the instructional team and, therefore, was similar to the Orange walk-through team, which included interim superintendent, assistant superintendent for curriculum and instruction, principal of Orange High School, assistant principals of Orange High School, director, cabinet members—director of special education, director of curriculum and testing all principals, all supervisors, all coaches, Mr. Robert Markel, president of the Orange Education Association, and Ms. Mary Karem, vice president of the Orange Teachers Association.

Since mutual respect between the teacher and the coach is the cornerstone of the EICM, a significant amount of time was devoted to developing trusting relationships with members of the instructional team at each of our schools. Our experience reinforced our understanding that trusting relationships evolve over a period time. It became clear to each instructional coaching team that all meaningful relationships that developed were the result of their actions and behaviors and not simply what they said or wrote.

Our first instructional coaching team (ICT) initiative began at Orange High School with the Orange High School Math Department. The ICT informed the mathematics department that our expectation was to provide instructional coaching for the purpose of enhancing and supporting their efforts as classroom instructors. Our goal was to improve the level and quality of instruction. The expected outcome was a greater number of their math students would attain proficient and advanced-proficient scores on local and state assessments.

A Power Point was presented, which outlined our intentions, emphasizing a system of support and reviewing the strategies of the EICM. This PowerPoint presented research that student learning is more effective when students engage in inquiry-based models that emphasize critical thinking and independent learning. A discussion followed, which described inquiry-based learning as an approach driven by questions posed by learners. After dialoguing back and forth, we reached a consensus that in many cases, the teachers' role is to guide students in finding answers to their questions and to encourage students to ask new questions that have meaning to them. We discussed the findings from the inquiry-based learning study completed by the Fayetteville Schools. This study revealed evidence that when students choose their own questions, they were motivated to learn and develop a sense of ownership (Inquiry Based Learning NSBA youtube.com). http://www.com/watch?v=z5MfyE-E

This conversation was followed with a discussion on the findings of the increase in student achievement at Orange Middle School, confirmed by the Mid-Atlantic Compliance Center, the federal overseers of No Child Left Behind. Among the handouts that were distributed was information on the reform strategies. We acknowledge that the reform strategies were the impetus behind this achievement, and we expected extensive use of them for this initiative. We emphasized that other inquiry-based strategies that resulted in proficient or advanced-proficient learning would be welcomed and acceptable. The instructional coaching team was introduced to the math team. We entertained questions from the mathematics department and set the stage to begin instructional coaching. OHS Mathematics Department accepted our challenge. Their initial reaction indicated that they were delighted that their department was selected. We left the meeting feeling very excited about this important instructional initiative. On several occasions, we received phone calls to discuss items found from the literature that were handed out and we had follow-up meetings to clarify the initiative.

Members of the Orange High School administrative team, the assistant superintendent for curriculum and instruction, director of testing, and I had an initial meeting to proceed with the initiative to provide instructional coaching to Orange High School's mathematics department. We defined instructional coaching as an instructional practice where the coach guides professional learning for teachers in a district, school, or classroom. As suggested by Darling-Hammond and Mclaughlin (1995), it is tailored to meet the needs identified by teachers and is an inquiry-based approach to learning.

We reviewed the components that we all agreed upon. The major goal of the classroom teacher was to create a setting that inspires his/her students to engage in critical thinking and independent learning. We would take measures to encourage the teacher that we were coaching to afford students as many opportunities as possible to engage in problem-solving activities to attain proficient and advanced-proficient results on skills stemming from the objectives that were taught. We made it clear that this was not content coaching. All content issues and concerns were referred to a mathematics specialist.

The second item on the agenda was for the coaches to understand we were going to attain our goal by encouraging teachers to employ instructional practices that encouraged teachers to instruct student-directed lessons and encouraged students to take responsibility for their learning. We carefully reviewed the strategies that the district had embraced over the past three years:

1. Accountable talk—the instructional practice involves teachers devoting a significant portion of their instructional time to solving problems related to core concepts.It requires teachers to be visionaries and to design instructional activities with the big picture or concept in mind. It requires teachers to create essential questions that inspire students to think and ask critical questions. The teacher is required to develop an atmosphere of trust where it is OK for students to make mistakes. The teachers must sharpen students' thinking by reinforcing their abilities to use and create knowledge. Teachers must press students for clarification or to explain or challenge a point of view or application of a solution. Teachers must ask students to restate or interpret what is said by another student, and finally, teachers must require students to probe a misconception or error.

2. Differentiated instruction—refers to the practice where the teacher takes measures that ensure that they address the variety of learning styles of the students in their classroom to make sure that the instruction is varied in such a way to accommodate the needs of all students assigned to the class. These accommodations are an infusion of all best instructional practices derived

from the major learning theories—if a student learns best from strategies associated with operant conditioning, then that student should have that benefit of that type of instruction; or if a student learns best as a result of instruction based upon brain-based instruction, then that student should have the benefit of that type of instruction. If a student learns best as a result of constructing knowledge, then that student should have an instructional activity that allows for that; and if students learn best by engaging in project-based activities, then that student should have the opportunity for inquiry-based learning. The accommodations can be as simplistic as restating a concept by using more advanced vocabulary or a more basic vocabulary, or it could mean increasing the use of technology.

3. Socratic questioning—is the practice whereby the teacher professes ignorance of the topic under discussion in order to elicit engaged dialogue with students. The teacher seeks to get the student that is asking the question to answer their own question by making them think out their own question. The six types of questions recognized as Socratic are conceptual clarification, probing, rationale reasoning and evidence, viewpoint and perspective, probing implications and consequences, and questions about questions.

4. Learning stations—are stationary or portable instructional centers that are designed around a particular unit of instruction. They offer challenging ways to learn and apply knowledge. Some classroom settings are designed as four learning stations or labs that require students to engage in a variety of cognitive skills that include listening, reading comprehension, scientific investigations, and critical thinking. Often, the design is infused with technology activities (i.e., tasks from websites or use and application of smart boards). Many times students are expected to apply their knowledge to a real-life problem or situation. Effective learning stations incorporate a level of rigor that will result in students gaining proficient or advanced-proficient skills.

5. Cooperative learning groups—refer to a practice where the teacher organizes their students into groups of four-to-five-member teams. According to Stahl (1992), Cooperative Learning Groups are a means to an end, rather than an end to themselves. Teachers must be precise when assigning tasks to students in each of the cooperative learning groups. They are expected to learn and to do well beyond the end of the group and the curriculum unit. All students are expected to buy into the targeted outcome, and the students must perceive these outcomes as their own. The students must accept that everyone in the group must master a common set of skills. Clear directions are given to students before they engage in their tasks. Heterogeneous groups have distinct advantages over homogeneous groups. They tend to become tolerant of diverse viewpoints, more considerate of others' thoughts and feelings. Members must come to the realization that they swim or sink as an academic team. All members of a team receive a reward or no members do.

Tasks are structured so that they must depend on each other. Over a period of time, members of groups learn interactive skills that include leadership, trust building, conflict management, constructive criticism, compromise, negotiation, and clarification. Teacher needs to assign specific roles to group members to make sure that they conscientiously work on specific behaviors. Teachers must structure the tasks so that students have access to comprehend specific information that they must learn. The content focus of learning must be aligned directly with specific outcome objectives and test items that will be used to measure these academic achievements.

6. Formative assessment—refers to the measures that teachers take to determine if students understand what is being taught. Periodically throughout the instructional block, the teacher should have students demonstrate that they understand the concepts being taught. The teacher must establish a set of signals that indicate that the instruction that is being taught is understood.

Proper application and implementation of EICM required an in-depth understanding of these definitions by the instructional staff and the instructional coaching team (ICT). This enabled everyone to be on the same page and ensured meaningful discussions and opportunities, instructional growth, and development. The instructional team was open to teachers employing other effective instructional practices as long as they encouraged students to engage in critical thinking, afforded students' opportunities to take responsibility for their learning, and led to proficient and advanced-proficient results.

It became clear that the only way that we could assure that all members of our team had clear and precise understanding of the five outlined instructional practices was to go into classrooms and observe these practices and return as a team and discuss the outcomes. We returned with some very interesting findings. We did not all have a clear understanding of the practices. Some of our actions disrupted classroom instruction. For example, one member did not understand the importance of giving a CLG uninterrupted time. This person would ask questions of students while the members of the CLG worked on their tasks. We also noted that some of the coaches did not understand the importance of taking comprehensive notes during an observation. All members of the ICT came to the realization that the observation involved in instructional coaching was quite different from the observations involved in walk-through. The ICT observation involved extensive and detailed note taking, and the latter does not. The ICT agreed that an effective technique for note taking was to record the time, the details of each instructional activity, and to include the transitional activity. The ICT learned to recognize the different learning styles that teachers used and how they result in effective or ineffective outcomes. The ICT discussed the instructional strategies until we reached consensus. The ICT agreed that we should look for Socratic questions throughout the instructional lesson—during the

Do Now; anticipatory set, which can be effectively accomplished via accountable talk; reinforcement activity, which can be effectively accomplished via CLGs; presentations made by students representing each CLG; and teacher summary of the lesson. The conversations and discussions of the ICT were helpful and led to all of us making adjustments. These efforts led to the development and improvement of the EICM.

The ICT had to make a commitment to this instructional initiative since we recognized how easy it was to allow our other professional responsibilities compromise the time that was required for this initiative to be successful. This meant it had to be added to our existing extensive professional responsibilities. When we met, we extended the same courtesy that we extended to the instructional staff to each other, and we were firmly committed to being a source of encouragement to each other. We reached consensus that every member was to be treated as an equal. This simple action led to an atmosphere that was analogous to that which we recommended to our instructional staff during "accountable talk" in their classrooms.

A third agenda item was to encourage the integration of technology into the teachers' instructional lessons. The ICT reviewed a statement presented in a paper by Educational Technology Support Center (ETSC) in 2005. Technology is only wise if it changes something about the way students learn, opens new doors and possibilities, and helps students engage in their learning experiences. If technology is used to make research projects, visual learning, collaborative groups, authentic learning projects, problem-solving and dynamic discussions happen, then it is used well. In essence, effective teachers integrate technology to facilitate learning and do not see it as an end unto itself. The ICT wanted to be clear on the measures that we suggested for the integration of technology into daily instruction. With the constant advancements being made in technology and our knowledge of our inventory, we agreed that we could expect our teachers to use smart boards, podcasting, use iPods, e-books, and have students visit learning websites. This expectation was based upon the recommendations of the technology coordinators and previous visits to classrooms throughout the district. ICT continued to meet regularly after specific instructional activities related to our instructional coaching activities with the selected math teachers.

Collaboration between the mathematic teachers and coaches resulted in the following conditions and the instructional items:

1. Follow the district's prescribed lesson plan format and understand the value of well-developed instructional lesson plans, and the teacher must start the process with a lesson plan that is designed with the end in mind.
2. Ask the big question—What is it that you want your students learn?
3. Follow the curriculum and the quarterly benchmark assessments prescribed by the district.

4. Be prepared to review the completed lesson plans with the coach from the perspective that the goal is to maximize instruction, with the understanding that the expectation of the coach is to observe inquiry-based or student-directed instruction from the beginning of the period until the end of the period and that the design of the instructional lesson affords students maximum opportunities for problem solving, critical thinking, independent learning, and accountability.

5. Understand that there are a number of methods and techniques that lead to effective instructional outcomes, and one possibility includes the following components—Do Now (appetizer), anticipatory set or presentation of the objectives, reinforcement activity, and summary, or use of an inquiry-based project for a unit of study for core or ancillary subjects.

6. Understand that pacing and transitioning are key elements for the delivery of effective instruction, and a designated amount of time must be allotted for each instructional activity, and this is accomplished seamlessly.

7. Present a brief overview of the lesson.

8. Understand that the Do Now should serve as a review and can be a problem(s) or Socratic question(s) from the previous day's instructional lesson. Consistency and routine are requirements for effective instruction. Students are to routinely repeat particular protocols until they become automatic and they include assigned seats; begin instructional lesson with Do Now; give students clear and succinct directions; train students to complete the Do Now instructional activity within three to five minutes; train students to offer solutions to the Do Now problem; evaluate and record results from Do Now. The teacher must recognize that this is a component of formative assessment and reinforces the importance of student and teacher accountability.

9. Understand that the anticipatory set or the presentation of the objectives follows the Do Now and is the heart of the instructional lesson, and employment of accountable talk is the recommended instructional strategy for accomplishing this instructional activity. The seating configuration must be configured so that there is a sense of trust between the students and the teacher. This can be accomplished in a horseshoe, traditional row or a cluster configuration. The teacher must make sure every student understands the objectives being taught. The teacher must ask Socratic questions and must encourage and inspire students to engage in critical thinking. Students must be encouraged to elicit their own questions on a given topic and be encouraged to find answers and/or solutions to these Socratic inquiries. During accountable talk, the students and the teacher are working collaboratively on inquiries related to the objectives. This is the time the teacher uses Socratic questions to present formulas, laws, hypotheses, theories definitions. This presentation must have authentic connections to the students' life at home or to their community and/or to the events taking place on a national level and/or on a

global level. This means the topics can include a mathematic-related problems associated with the 2011 Fukushima Daiichi Nuclear Plant disaster, Tohoku earthquake, and tsunami in Japan. The teacher must know the learning style of every student and employ differentiated instruction to ensure every student comprehends each objective. This includes giving the students an opportunity to solve a problem individually or as a collective group. As a measure of formative assessment, the teacher can visit each student. The teacher then decides if he or she should restate or clarify the concept by asking another Socratic question or offer an explanation. This activity should be completed within ten to fifteen minutes.

10. Understand that the reinforcement activity follows the anticipatory set and most of the instructional time should be devoted to this instructional activity. The teacher can assign students to work in pairs (Carolina Pairs). This affords the students the opportunity to defend their solution to a classmate. They must reach consensus. Both students benefit even when one student assumes the role of instructor. The Carolina Pairs can then collapse into cooperative learning groups (CLGs) made up of four members. The assigned tasks must reflect the appropriate level of rigor. The students are accustomed and familiar with the roles of the CLGM and follow the protocol of each role—team leader, team recorder, timekeeper, and team presenter. The activity is concluded with the team presenter explaining their solution to the other students. This activity can also be an inquiry-based project, which is assigned over several class periods. The team members of each CLG assist the team presenter with his or her explanation. The teacher guides students in completing a written summary, ensuring that the students understand the lesson objectives, have correct and pertinent data from each CLG presentation, and accurately record notes in student notebooks so that the concepts can be reviewed and referred to for a test, quiz, or future reference.

11. Train teachers to integrate local and/or world events into the anticipatory set. ICT must assist teacher in making authentic connections so that students naturally see the connections between what they are learning in the classroom and what is taking place in their lives at home, in their community, and/or in the world.

12. The ICT stressed that it was critical for teachers to ensure that everyone comprehended the objectives.

13. The ICT stressed that it was during the anticipatory set of the instructional lesson that teachers found it useful to employ Bloom's taxonomy and Gardner's multiple intelligences and engage in repetition for the auditory learners or bring in models or the equivalent to accommodate the visual learners or inspire critical thinking by employing the six types of Socratic questions—conceptual clarification, probing assumptions, probing rationale, reasons and evidence questions, questioning viewpoints and perspectives,

questions that probe implications and consequences, and questions about questions.

14. The ICT stressed that when employing accountable talk, the trust between the teacher and their students is a huge factor, and they noted the importance that this phase of the instructional lesson has upon the learning for the remainder of the instructional block. If the students don't understand the instructional objectives, they will have difficulty engaging in higher order activities that involve application, analysis, synthesis, and/or evaluation. The next phase of the instructional lesson is student engagement in the reinforcement activity. Rigor or an element of challenge and/or sophistication is an important factor—the ICT stressed that this portion of the lesson can't be overly simple nor can it be overly sophisticated that only a few in the class comprehend it. The teacher must take every student into account and make learning not only interesting but vital. This should to be accomplished within ten to fifteen minutes.

15. The teacher must be open to the ideas that students are extremely bright and realize that there are a number of different solutions to a given task. The teacher must not only maintain an open mind but encourage this kind of critical thinking.

16. The ICT stressed that teachers had to understand that students are responsible for their learning and the reinforcement activity is to be accomplished via the CLGM. The teacher must design tasks that reflected an appropriate level of rigor and afford opportunities to problem-solve through the collaborative efforts of a team. The teacher must promote students to engage in individualized tasks as well as group tasks as part of the experience. The tasks must include activities that inspired students to gain knowledge, comprehend data, apply learned knowledge to problems, engage in analysis of data, synthesize data, and/or evaluate data and make comparisons.

17. These tasks must be designed to include the six types of Socratic questions. The ICT must encourage the use of websites or smart boards, video games, iPods notebook computers, texting, and all the technology that is available to young people. The ICT must encourage the teachers to recognize that the experience must teach students how to recognize individual talents as well as group talents and stressed that while learning academic skills, the students also develop good character-building traits, which teach students to be inclusive and appreciative of others students' talents and disabilities. This usually requires the teacher to make adjustments to the tasks that are suggested in textbooks or websites.

18. The ICT also stressed that the experience of effective CLGs improved students' speaking skills and their level of confidence. The ICT stressed that teachers give their students ten to fifteen minutes of uninterrupted time for this activity.

19. ICT stressed that teachers understand that the presentations of each CLG serves as an excellent measure for the summary of the instructional lesson. The ICT stressed that the teacher has a responsibility to make sure that their students see the connections between the anticipatory set or the teacher's presentation of the objectives, the findings reached by each presenter of each CLG. The teachers are trained to highlight and summarize information that they want their students to retain.

20. The instructional coach and the teacher review all aspects of the teacher's lesson, making sure that all elements reflect student-directed instruction.

21. Close attention was given to the level of rigor and the pacing of each instructional activity.

22. The coach and the teacher used Bloom's taxonomy to determine the level of rigor of the activities that are included in their instructional lesson plans. They ask the question, "Did the activity included lead to the attainment of

- knowledge—in other words, was the teacher asking students to arrange, define, duplicate, label, or recall data?
- understanding—was the teacher asking the student to classify, describe, discuss, explain, identify, locate, recognize, restate, or translate data?
- application—was the teacher asking the student to apply, choose, demonstrate, employ, illustrate, interpret, operate, practice, sketch, solve, use, or write data?
- analysis—was the teacher asking the students to analyze, appraise, calculate, categorize, compare, contrast, criticize, differentiate, distinguish, examine, experiment, question, test data?
- synthesis—was the teacher requiring the students to arrange, assemble, collect, compose, construct, create, design, develop, formulate, manage, organize, plan, prepare, propose, set up, or write data?
- evaluation—was the teacher asking students to appraise, argue, assess, attach, choose, compare, defend, estimate, judge, predict, rate, select, support, value, or evaluate data?"

23. Most importantly, was the teacher requiring the students to engage in a combination of the above operations?

24. These rigorous instructional tasks involving mathematic teachers discussing their instructional lessons as it related to concepts of various instructional models assisted them in recognizing that textbooks should be employed as one resource and not the only resource.

25. The coaches made it clear that they were looking for specific examples of accountable talk, Socratic questions, differentiated instruction, CLGs, learning stations; and when the instructional lesson lacked these instructional strategies, the coach and the teacher reviewed the instructional lesson to

determine if the inclusion of these instructional strategies would lead to more effective instruction.

26. Lastly, the coach and the teacher reviewed the instructional lesson to determine if instruction involved had application to real-life situations, which students encounter in their day-to-day activities, or had relevance to the world that they will inherit.

My idea of education is to unsettle the minds of
the young and inflame their intellects.

—Robert Maynard Hutchins

Instructional Coaching

I met with the teacher, whom I coached on a one-to-one basis, for the first time; and although we both had been part of meetings where the purpose for the instructional coaching was introduced, I reiterated that I was involved with this initiative to support this teacher's efforts as they relate to classroom instruction and that the goal was to encourage teachers of the mathematics department to provide student-directed instruction. I explained the focus of the coaching was to examine the components or elements of the instructional lesson and see if altering one or more of these elements would improve the delivery of instruction. I made it clear that I was not a mathematics expert and that if any of the teachers requested assistance on math content, experts were available. We set a date for my first visit. This visit was designed to become familiar with the teacher's setting—the room where the teacher taught, the students, and the learning environment. The class met for eighty-two minutes. The first observation, I visited for approximately forty minutes, and I made it clear that I was there just to become acquainted with the teacher and the assigned algebra students. Before our next meeting, this teacher visited a representative of the teachers' association. The question to the union representative was, did I have the right to visit this teacher's mathematics class? The teacher was told that I had this right. This reiterated the importance of a coach developing a trusting relationship with the teacher being coached.

Our second meeting was a postobservation to prepare for the next observation and to discuss the first observation. We began with small talk, exchanging general information. I shared some of the positive information that had been passed on to me about this mathematic teacher's style of teaching, which emphasized the excellent rapport that this teacher had with his/her students. This teacher had a reputation of caring and sharing, and this was communicated during this conference. This teacher informed me that these acts of kindness that I referred to led to his/her being assigned some of the most challenging students in the school. Effective teachers often report similar claims.

I informed this teacher that on my initial visit, I observed evidence of caring attitude and noted that this teacher seemed to be everywhere and every place for these algebra students. I asked this teacher about the composition of this class and learned that it was quite a challenging situation, with several students who only spoke

French, and some of these students had recently come to our school district from Haiti and had a very limited mathematics background.

My next question was to ask this teacher for his/her meaning of student-directed instruction. The response was a high level of student engagement and students taking responsibility for their own learning. Then I asked this teacher if this had taken place in the class that I had observed, and this teacher looked at me and asked the same question of me. My response was for us to examine my observation notes, which included this teacher writing the appetizer or the Do Now on the board; I noted that the teacher received limited responses and this teacher took responsibility for writing the solution, asked follow-up questions, and proceeded to visit every student in the class to offer assistance. This teacher and I agreed that he/she had done most of the work while his/her students had made minimum effort in assuming responsibility for their learning. The teacher stated that he/she employed to the style of teaching to accommodate the students' limited understanding and use of the English language.

I asked this teacher if we could design some measures to move from a teacher-directed style of instruction to a student-directed style of instruction. The teacher agreed, and we proceeded to develop a plan. The first instructional item that we addressed was the seating configuration. The students sat haphazardly throughout the classroom. We discussed the negative impact that this was having upon instruction, and the teacher agreed to address this problem immediately. The teacher changed the random seating configuration of the students to a traditional configuration of rows. We discussed how this configuration worked well for the Do Now and for the anticipatory set. Later, this teacher would include pairs and quads as part of his/her seating configuration.

The teacher and I discussed the importance of limiting the appetizer to three to five minutes, and we then discussed measures that he/she could implement for greater student participation. The method employed during the first observation inspired limited student participation. Student volunteers were not required to write and/or explain the solution to the problem to the teacher or their classmates. Another very important observation that was discussed with this teacher was the extended time that was allotted for the appetizer. We discussed how this compromised the instructional time needed for the other instructional activities. A brief discussion of rigor was also introduced into this conversation. It was noted that rigor is compromised when students do not assume responsibility for their learning.

This mathematics teacher asked interesting questions. However, since whole-group instruction was employed for the entire instructional block, the questions remained in the range of knowledge and understanding on Bloom's taxonomy. The teacher's style of instruction offered the students limited opportunities to problem-solve. Most of the solutions were completed by the teacher. The other concern that I reported was related to formative assessment. Since this teacher took few opportunities to find out if the objectives were understood, this teacher faced the difficulty of not knowing if the students understood the objectives presented.

During this postconference, I asked this teacher to employ CLGM for our next observation, and the teacher stated that the students were not ready for CLGM but stated that he/she would employ the Carolina Pairs Model.

This teacher and I concluded our postobservation, accomplishing the following:

> March 9 was our date for the next coaching observation, and I would observe the algebra class for the complete eighty-two-minute block.
>
> The lesson plan was well developed and followed the district's lesson plan format and included an appetizer, which required students to identify two procedures used for adding and subtracting polynomials. The objective was for all students to understand the meaning of a binomial expression and to be able to solve word problems related to the area of a rectangle.
>
> The students were asked to determine the area of a lawn and had to understand that

Area of Lawn = Total Area – Area of House – Area of Driveway

The teacher decided the reinforcement activity was, the students would complete examples of binomial expressions using the Carolina Pairs Model.

Because of our time limitations, part of our time was used for preconference discussion. The teacher requested me to look closely at the following instructional activities: the appetizer, the transition into the anticipatory set, and the transition into the Carolina Pairs. Most importantly, the mathematics teacher agreed that it was in the best interest of the students to design Socratic questions related to polynomials, which involved application of the rules; and finally, we agreed that the students via Carolina Pairs would present their solutions to their classmates.

I left the preconference, feeling very good about our progress.

March 9, 2010, Observation

On the date of the second observation, I arrived shortly before the instructional block began. My copy of the teacher's instructional lesson plan matched the instructional lesson plan that this teacher and I had agreed upon at the preconference. Further, the plan coincided with the pacing guide, the quarterly benchmark assessments, and the NJCCCS. I immediately noticed the climate in this classroom had greatly improved. Comparing the two observations, a more positive feeling emanated from the students during this observation as compared to during my first observation. On this occasion, students were more focused on algebra instruction.

The students gathered in the back of the classroom, reviewing a posting of the points that they had earned for completing a math activity from the previous day, which involved the use of the Carolina Pairs Model. These students were highly motivated by this reward system, and it carried over into their instructional lesson.

The first instructional activity that was designed to be graded as a quiz, the appetizer, was a problem that had been taught the previous day. While a greater number of students offered responses to the solution, many of the students did not participate in attaining the solution. The entire instructional activity took less than five minutes.

The mathematics teacher smoothly transitioned from the appetizer to the anticipatory set. The objective was, 100 percent of the algebra students will master the skills involved in adding and subtracting polynomials. Accountable talk was employed to attain this objective. The students appeared to understand the concepts; however, I noted that it would have been useful for the teacher to ask fewer objective questions and more Socratic questions. I noted that an excessive number of hints were given to the students, and this appeared to compromise the students' motivation to engage in critical thinking.

The students quickly transitioned into Carolina Pairs for their reinforcement activity. The ease of their movement into the Carolina Pairs illustrated their level of comfort and familiarity with this model. The expectation was that they would demonstrate their skills of adding and subtracting polynomials. There seem to be a disconnection between the anticipatory set and the reinforcement activity.

I noted the students did not have a clear understanding of the expectations. The directions should have been clear and concise (i.e., Use your textbooks and notes to solve the problem. State what the type of polynomial and explain each step that you employed to attain your answer.)

I noted that the students would have benefited from being reminded to read and review the rules for adding and subtracting polynomials.

In addition, I noted that it appeared that the students would have benefited from knowing the amount of time they had to complete this task.

Postconference of April 9 Instructional Coaching Observation

The mathematics teacher and I had established a more trusting relationship and spoke freely to each other. I informed him/her that I was impressed with the classroom climate. The majority of his/her students' behavior changed from passive to enthusiastic. The increased level of student engagement and student motivation indicated that students responded positively to the reward system of the Carolina Pairs Model. There was improvement in the implementation of the appetizer. An item of constructive criticism was that a student or students, and not the teacher, should have written the solution to the problem on the board. By not doing so, the teacher passed up an opportunity for her students to demonstrate their problem-solving skills.

The use of accountable talk during the anticipatory set was effective. I informed this teacher that I believed that quality of their instruction would have benefited from including more Socratic questions during this phase of their instructional lesson. We specifically concentrated on questions that require the students to provide rationale, reasons, and evidence for solutions to algebra problems. We specifically related these to the teachers-objective of adding and subtracting polynomials. We discussed the importance of students acquiring the skills involved in application of a rule. The students did not appear to be able to make a clear association between that rule presented during the anticipatory set and the rule that they were expected to apply during the reinforcement activity, as demonstrated during the reinforcement activity which involved the use of the Carolina Pairs Model. The mathematics teacher discussed measures that she had designed in her lesson plans for clarifying the directions of each task. After a discussion, the teacher and I agreed that the students would have benefited from mastering the given application before they were introduced to a new application.

There was great improvement in the pace of the lesson, and this math teacher was pleased with the measures that he/she had taken. By carefully timing each instructional activity, he/she attained the desired outcome. This discussion also included the mathematics teacher's excellent utilization of the Carolina Pairs Model. He/she had developed a strategy to accommodate the unique challenges of her non-English-speaking students. He/she paired the students in a pattern that afforded all students the opportunity to learn from each other. It was noted that both parties benefited from this arrangement, those being assisted and those who assisted. The teacher had put a great deal of effort to maximize learning for all the students, and the instructional activity reflected this.

Preconference for May 14 Instructional Coaching Observation

The mathematics teacher came prepared with a well-developed instructional lesson, which followed all district requirements. His/her plans reflected more choices of instructional activities that would lead to student-directed learning. Her lesson plan design reflected that this teacher took the following suggestions into consideration:

- The instructional planning began with the big idea in mind.
- He/she clearly described what he/she wanted the assigned students to learn during the instructional block. During the previous instructional lesson, the coach observed appropriate time was not allotted for a summary of the instructional lesson.
- The teacher wrote down the essential questions that would be used for each component of the instructional lesson.
- The appetizer was designed as a formative assessment measure—the teacher gave her students five minutes to complete a problem that was to be graded as a quiz; it required one student to write the solution and another student to offer an explanation.

- The math teacher designed the anticipatory set to be presented via accountable talk. The math teacher decided to raise the level of rigor by requiring students to include math vocabulary in their responses.
- The reinforcement activity was designed to elevate the critical thinking skills for all the assigned students. The mathematics teacher had taken time to read and included an article entitled the "Collaborative Classroom" by Tinzmann, Jones, Fennimore, Bakker, Fine, Pierce, and Brook (1990). This article affirmed the importance of moving from a mind-set of a traditional classroom, where the teacher is viewed as the information giver, to the mind-set of a collaborative classroom, where knowledge is shared.
- The mathematics teacher identified with the role of the collaborative teacher and saw how instruction could be elevated by building upon the knowledge, personal experiences, language, strategies, and culture of the students assigned to the algebra class. The instructional lesson plans included an instructional strategy that mathematics teacher referred to as the 1-2-4 activity.
- The teacher selected four problems that involved the multiplication of polynomials. The mathematics teacher's plans required the students to work independently.
- After three minutes, the students were required to discuss their independent work with a teammate—in this case, their Carolina Pair.
- The activity was designed to continue with the Carolina Pairs collapsing into quads for a final discussion of the solution.
- The mathematics teacher's instructional lesson plan concluded with the presenter from each quad presenting a solution to each of the four problems. The mathematics teacher's lesson plan included a summary of the instructional lesson.

May 14 Instructional Coaching Observation

The instructional lesson was quite a departure from the first instructional lesson observed on March 23. The mathematics teacher followed the instructional plan that was reviewed. The first indication that this instructional lesson was more rigorous than previous lessons observed was the students' use of mathematic vocabulary. The first concept noted was a discussion involving the concept of a "discriminant." The student understood the use of the term and used it freely when offering a solution to the appetizer, which again was graded as a quiz. There was greater use of formative assessment during each component of the lesson. The mathematics teacher requested a show of hands to determine how many students had included the term *discriminant* as part of their solution. Six students responded. The mathematics teacher informed the students that this was good a practice, using information from their notes when seeking a solution to a problem. The teacher demonstrated excellent use of the Socratic questioning by asking one of the six students to explain the meaning of *discriminant*. This offered the students an opportunity to hear another perspective of the concept. This indicated that the mathematics teacher understood the importance of Socratic questions.

During the anticipatory set, via accountable talk, this mathematics teacher employed more effective measures of communication. The teacher linked the mathematics problem to an experience that the students encountered in their daily lives. The new information that was taught was linked to prior knowledge. While the students engaged in rich conversation as they completed a problem requiring them to multiply polynomials, the mathematics teacher visited every student. Although he/she only made brief comments to the students, it was clear that this monitoring technique served as an important tool for improving instruction. Judging from the expressions on the students' faces, it appeared to boost their confidence and made them feel connected.

The 1-2-4 activity was employed effectively during the reinforcement component of the instructional lesson. The students were required to complete one of four problems involving the multiplication of polynomials. As implied by this technique, the students first worked independently for three minutes. This gave each student some time to think independently and creatively. During the next phase of this instructional activity, the students joined their Carolina Pairs Partner and discussed their independent findings. The objective was to determine if their colleague agreed or disagreed with the solution that had reached. The instructional activity was successful; the students agreed with each other in some cases and challenged their classmates in other situations. The next phase was to collapse the Carolina Pairs into quads so that class ended up in groups of fours. Since this class was familiar with the CLGM, they transitioned with ease and quickly assumed the roles so that each of the four groups could present their findings. The objective was to reach consensus on a solution and to present and explain their findings to the class. The students had embraced this style of learning. The presenters from each of the quads were able to clearly and succinctly present their findings. The mathematics teacher facilitated the summary of the lessons via the findings presented by each student presenter. The teacher gave specific directions as to what the students were required to include as part of their notes. The students were told that they would be quizzed the following day on the multiplication of polynomials. One advantage to this type of collaborative learning is that students increase the amount of knowledge learned by as much as 75 percent. By allowing students to present their findings, the mathematics teacher encouraged students to recognize that there are several ways of arriving at a solution to a problem.

Instructional coaching had a powerful impact upon this particular algebra class. Initially, the majority of their instruction was teacher-directed learning and included passive learning, which required minimum use of problem-solving skills. When this mathematics teacher transitioned to student-directed learning, the students began to engage in critical and creative thinking and then to developed opinions based on their understanding and interpretation of skills being taught. From the 1-2-4 activity, the students were afforded the opportunity to embrace a model that led them to become familiar with independent and creative thinking and involved in the important skill of being a collaborative member of a CLG. They learned to defend their positions and were given opportunities to agree or disagree with their classmates. This experience helped the students to work with other students who had diverse opinions and backgrounds, which included learning to respect one another's differences. The reward system was an important component of this model and enabled the students to attain a positive perspective on collaboration and excited their competitive spirit. Since a portion of the students' grade was based upon the collaborative work of the entire team, the daily rewards motivated them to have a vested interest in their learning experience.

Another important lesson gained from this experience was everyone learned from everyone. It was noted that the teacher's astute knowledge of these algebra students enabled this teacher to organize the Carolina Pairs and the quads in a manner that balanced the skills, talents, and challenges of the assigned students of this algebra class. This was accomplished without any embarrassment. The French-speaking students translated for non-English-speaking students and consequently, the non-English-speaking began to respond in English. The mathematics teacher went from the role of a traditional teacher to a modern-day educator who facilitates learning. This mathematics teacher developed the skill of giving these algebra students hints or cues via use of Socratic questioning. These questions or cues sometimes led to providing students with feedback or redirecting a question so the students began to view the problems from different perspectives. When it was necessary, the teacher asked questions of the team leader, which energized this student to provide better leadership. By the end of this experience, these algebra students were assuming greater responsibility for their learning.

The other members of our ICT had similar experiences. The use of Bloom's taxonomy became a major instructional resource tool for one of our coaches and this teacher. The teacher taught Algebra II, and the coach was a former mathematics teacher. During the initial preconference, the coach asked the teacher what he wanted assistance with. The teacher's response was to inspire his students to become more motivated and engaged in classroom participation. The coach noted that the teacher came to the preconference prepared with his instructional lesson plan, which met all district requirements. The coach's first question to the teacher was, do you have high expectations of your students? The teacher's response was that he did. The coach explained the importance of teachers having high expectations of his students and continued the conversation by making reference to literature on this topic including Edmonds's "Effective Schools" (1985), Levin's Accelerated Schools Program (1997), and Slavin's Success for All Project (1996). It was mentioned that the latter project demonstrated that engaging low-achieving students in a challenging curriculum accelerated academic and social outcomes. This was in direct contrast to the dismal achievement of students, whose schools labeled them slow learners and tracked them to low-ability classes, and it was noted that a high percentage of these students were students of color. Initially, this teacher did not see any connection between the discussion of this literature and their students. This teacher pointed out that his students were in Algebra II, which is an advanced mathematics course.

The coach suggested to use Bloom's taxonomy as an instructional tool to gain insight into possible solutions and to reference their discussion. The teacher agreed, and they carefully reviewed the instructional activities that the teacher selected for the students involved to facilitate the learning of quadratic equations. They concluded that if these instructional activities were categorized into Bloom's taxonomy, they would fall into range of remembering, understanding, and applying.

Shortly thereafter, the coach visited this Algebra II class to become familiar with the teacher's learning style and the climate of this particular class. The coach observed that the students spent the majority of their time solving quadratic equations and the related functions with limited enthusiasm or focus. They appeared to be putting forth minimal effort. During this visit, the coach observed that the many of the students appeared to be more interested in playing video games on their cell phones than they were in the Algebra II instruction. The coach noticed that when the students were asked to put their video games away, they did so without any argument or confusion. However, whenever an opportunity arose, they would return their attention to the video games.

The coach asked the teacher what his/her feelings were regarding the students' desire to play video games during class time. The teacher's response was that he/she viewed this practice as a distraction and that the video games had little intellectual value, especially when one compares this practice to the instructional activities that he/she prepared for these students on a daily basis. The coach continued this conversation about video games, and the conversation went from the video games having little value to having some value. The coach asked, "Was it possible to use the video games to raise the level of motivation of these students?" After going back and forth about the use of the video games, the teacher stated that he/she had noticed that the students used problem-solving skills when they played their video games. The teacher went on to say that he/she noticed that some students used highly advanced critical-thinking skills when they challenge themselves to play the video games without the knowledge of the rules and that winning the game required the students to simultaneously solve for two variables.

As the preconference continued, the teacher and the coach brainstormed on techniques that could be used to motivate these Algebra II students. The coach encouraged the teacher to place greater value on critical thinking, such as that which can be attained from the student engagement with video games, and referred to what Gardner (1985) said: "Teachers who teach to a broad range of learning styles and multiple intelligences communicate that the school values the unique strengths and intelligences of each individual." This conversation also made mention that "schools that motivate young people to learn do not rely on standardized tests that assess one or two types of intelligences, usually linguistic and logical-mathematical" Gardner (1985). Bernard stated "Nor do they focus on the 'right answer' questions and assessments." Instead, they use several assessment approaches—including authentic assessments that promote student reflection, critical inquiry, and problem solving—and assessments that validate children's different intelligences, strengths, and learning styles (Bernard, 1995).

The teacher decided, and the coach agreed that he could increase the level of engagement of his students by organizing the instruction into three categories: analyzing, evaluating, and creating by coupling these categories with activities that motivate students in their daily activities. The teacher decided that he would include video games as part of this unit.

Shortly thereafter, the teacher designed a lesson plan that focused on the understanding and the application of quadratic equations that included the use of video games. The teacher identified the skills that the students would learn in the traditional fashion, including completing the square, and the skills required for learning the quadratic formula to solve quadratic equations. According to Bloom's taxonomy, the skills involved the categories of remembering, understanding, and applying. The second set of lesson plans on this topic involved a nontraditional approach, which required students to design a video game that was based upon the quadratic equation. The teacher required the students to use skills, which, according to the categories of Bloom's taxonomy, include analyzing, evaluating, and creating. The teacher created a reward system that prohibited the use of video games until the students had mastered the first set of skills. With the use of cell phones and classroom computers, students created video games based upon the quadratic equation and then analyzed and evaluated their project.

The teacher used the design and activities of video games to motivate these students to master the benchmark skills and assessments outlined in the quarterly benchmark and assessment resource tools for Algebra II. The students bought into this style of learning because they saw it as real-life activities that have implications in their world. The students realized that there were many solutions to problems as they moved up Bloom's taxonomy model, and by the end of the experience, the students were creating video games that matched the open-ended format style question found on the state mathematics assessment.

Using technology in this manner heightened the students' motivation for the unit of study of quadratic equations. The students stated that they felt the teacher respected their interests and they were able to make real-life connections between learning mathematics and video games.

The great difficulty in education is to get experience out of ideas.

—George Santayana

The Education Instructional Coaching Model

It is fair to say that school reform in the Orange Public School District made significant gains as a result of its affiliation with the Institute for Research and Reform in Education (IRRE). Redesigning our secondary schools into the First Things First model of small communities began with the premise that we wanted a model that could raise the academic performance for all students, including those with troubled academic histories to levels required for postsecondary education and for successful entry into the job market.

A significant amount of time is devoted to developing trusting relationships with the staff since mutual respect between the teacher and the coach is the cornerstone of the Education Instructional Coaching Model (EICM). The model is introduced to the staff as a separate entity and not part of the formal evaluative process. When properly implemented, it will not be long before the instructional coaching team (ICT) realizes that when they joined forces with teachers and systematically observe classroom practices, academic achievement will improve.

The instructional lessons that the participating teachers prepare must reflect that they are designed to inspire students to become critical thinkers and independent learners. These lessons must afford students numerous opportunities to engage in problem-solving activities and to attain proficient and advanced-proficient results.

Both parties must agree that they will concentrate on the reform strategies: Socratic questioning, accountable talk, formative assessment, differentiated instruction, cooperative learning groups, and learning stations. Together, they meet for pre-conferences, observations, and post conferences. During the preconference, the teachers present lesson plans that include numerous opportunities for student engagement, acceptable levels of rigor, and offer students opportunities to take responsibility for their learning. During the observations, the ICT takes copious notes to assist teachers in determining if they are applying the best instructional practices for teaching specific instructional objectives, which they selected, designed, or are required. At postconference, teachers and members of the ICT discuss the areas of strengths and areas that they want to improve or want assistance with. Collaboratively, the coach and the teacher develop strategies and techniques to address these areas of concern. Preconference dates are scheduled, and thus, the process continues until all instructional goals are achieved.

Improving instruction is hard work and is always accompanied by challenges. It was not uncommon for staff to revert back to teacher-directed instruction. Nor was it uncommon for coaches to alter a component of the EICM and, thus, compromise student outcome. These setbacks often occurred after scheduled disruption (i.e., a special event that requires staff to alter their daily routine). On occasion, when the ICT visited classrooms after special events, they noted the negative impact it had upon the implementation of the EICM. The ICTs were well aware of these occurrences and were always prepared to go back to the drawing board and review the components of the model with the instructional staff. We learned that recovery was easily attainable with small group conversations and or written suggestions on the lessons plans. This resulted in an expedient recovery.

Similarly, we were equally surprised by positives. Once we were in the midst of a workshop, somehow the concept Socratic method was mentioned. The staff became so engrossed with the topic that they requested that the facilitator offer them a workshop on Socratic questioning. The teachers actually made all of the professional development arrangements.

Too often we give children answers to remember rather than problems to solve.

—Roger Levin

Summary of Education Instructional Coaching Model

The Education Instructional Coaching Model is summarized as a model that can be used by a school or a district that is interested in having effective schools or "smart schools," which afford every student opportunities to engage in critical thinking and be independent, proficient, and advanced-proficient learners. The model requires the following:

1. The central office of the school district to take measures that ensure every member or stakeholder within the school district and community is committed to school reform.
2. Central office takes measures to data driven by assessment data.
3. Schools must organized into small learning communities or similar organizational models.
4. The central office of the district to establish quarterly benchmarks and assessments that are aligned with state standards, which enables every school in the district to monitor what students are being taught and what they have mastered.
5. To have a clear understanding of effective classroom strategies, including but not limited to, the reform strategies: Socratic questioning, accountable talk, differentiated instruction, formative assessment, cooperative group learning model, Bloom's taxonomy, Gardner's multiple intelligences, and rigor.
6. Committed teachers, who are willing to write effective lesson plans using effective models (i.e., Understanding by Design).
7. Teachers who are willing to deliver student-directed lessons and devote most of their instruction time to students engaging in problem-solving activities.
8. An administrative team that is willing to serve as a support system for their instructional team and believes instructional coaching is the cornerstone for school reform.
9. Development of instructional coaching teams that are willing to take measures to coach teachers in such a way that they understand the connections between

lesson plan, the objectives, the Do Now, the anticipatory set, the reinforcement activity (via cooperative learning groups), and lesson summary.

10. To develop ICT that are committed to monitoring all instructional activities that take place in a classroom to ensure that teachers advance instruction that promotes the examination and implementation of educational models, which inspire students to engage in critical thinking and independent learning on a daily basis.

11. To develop ICT that utilizes a cycle involving a preconference and postconference until all teachers in a school district deliver instruction that enables all students to offer critical solutions to problems and earn proficient and advanced-proficient scores on local, state, and international assessments and, more importantly, enable students to become lifelong learners that can compete with their global counterparts, whether they are from China or Norway.

My parents told me "Finish your dinner People in China and India are starving."
I tell my daughters "Finish your homework People in China and India are
starving for your job."

—Thomas L. Freidman

CONCLUSION

The Education Instructional Coaching Model (EICM), which is based upon two components, reform strategies and instructional coaching, is a K–12 model that qualifies as the type of model that President Obama referred to in the January 28, 2011, State of the Union speech, an effort to "race to the top." He stated, "I will promote world-class academic standards and curriculum that fosters critical thinking, problem solving and the innovative knowledge to prepare students for college and career." He stated that he will push to end the use of ineffective, "off the shelf" tests and support new state-of-the-art assessment and accountability systems, which provide timely and useful information about learning and progress of individual students. The president also stated that all states should make improvements in teacher effectiveness and ensure that all schools have highly qualified teachers. There are very few professional development plans that offer structured measures for achieving this vital component of school reform.

Further, similar to the president, EICM believes "teachers are the single most important resource to a child's learning." This model acknowledges teachers as professionals while presenting an instructional tool, which assures that they are accountable. If EICM is properly implemented, it can enable American students in public or private schools to attain high standards, which will result in students being successful in our colleges and in their chosen careers.

The author recommends the use of the EICM for teacher preparatory programs at colleges and universities. Students deserve teachers prepared to provide instruction that will result in them becoming critical thinkers and independent learners.

WORKS CITED

Bakker, J., Fennimore, J., Fine, C., Pierce, J., Tinzmann, T. F., (1990). What is the Collaborative Classroom? retrieved March 2, 2009, from http: www.arp.spmet.org/adm/supt/collab2.htm-Cached

Bernard, M.P., Characteristics of Dissimilar Learners (1995). retrieved March 24, 2009, from http: www.education.com)...) Learning Disabilities—Cached

Bolak, K., Bialach, D. & Duhnphy, M. (2005) Standards-based Thematic Units that Integrate Units The Arts and Energize Students and Teachers Middle School Journal, 31 (2) 57-60

Brumfield, R Grants encourage sustainable tech. (2005). retrieved September 8, 2010 from http://www.esd112.org/edtech/sustainableclass.cfm.., eSchool News Online.

Carroll, T., & Fulton, K., (2004). The True Cost of Teacher Turnover [Electronic Version] Current Issue in Education Volume 8, Number 14, Threshold, 8-11, 15...

Connell, J.P., Klem, A. (2004) Relationships Matter: Linking Teacher Support to Students Engagement And Achievement. Journal of School Health, 74 (7) 262-273.

Darling-Hammond, L. & McLaughlin, M.W. (1995, April) Policies that support professional development in an era of reform. Phi Delta Kappan, 76(8) 597-604

Edmonds, R., (1985). History of Effective Schools Movement retrieved April 8, 2010 from www.lakeforest.edu../effective -schools/history of Effective schools...Cached Ronald R. Edmonds

Educational Technology Support Center (ETSC) (2005). What is the Sustainable Classroom? retrieved March 16, 2011 from http://www.esd112.org/edtech/sustainableclass.cfm

Fayetteville Schools Inquiry-based Learning retrieved March 2, 2011 from www.youtube.com/watch?v=z5MfyE-E Uploaded by NSBB market

Fosten, C., Grant, J., & Hollas, J., (2002). How to Differentiate Instruction in Mixed-ability Classrooms retrieved May 7, 2010 from http://www.lookstein.org/online_journal.php?id=107

Fosnot, C. (1996) Constructivism: A Psychological Theory of Learning Conservatism: Theory Perspectives And Practice New York: Teacher College Press, 8-33.

Gardner, H., (1985) The Mind's New Science: A History of the Cognitive Revolution. New York: Basic Books retrieved February 9, 2011 www. p z.harvard.edu/pis/HGpubs.htm

Heider, K.L. (2005) How Monitoring Programs Can Help Current Issues in Education, (8) 14, retrieved June 8, 2010 from http://cie.edasu.edu/vol8/number14

Levin, H.M. (1987) Accelerated schools for disadvantaged students, Educational Leadership, 44(6) 19-21.

Miller-Jacobs, S. , Differentiated Instruction: A Primer The Lookstein Center http://www.lookstein.org/online_journal.php?id=107

The National Commission of Excellence in Education, (1983). A Nation At Risk Report, retrieved January 10, 2011 from www.2.ed.gov/pubs/NatAtRisk Cached Oct. 7, 1999—The prominent 1983 report on America education from the National Commission of Excellence in Education.

Obama, B President of the United States (2011) State of the Union Address-Race to the Top, retrieved Jasnuary 27 2011 Released by the White House retrieved March 2, 2011 from http:www.fostercity.patch.com.articles/transcript-president-barack-obamas-state-of-the union-a...

Sammon, G. (2008) Creating and Sustaining Small Learning Communities Srtategies for Transforming High Schools. Corwin Press. 1-14

Skinner, B. F., (1984). The Shame of American Education retrieved October 5, 2008 from www.4shared.com/document/YTp6iBtQSkinner_B_1984_The_shame_o.html

Slavin, R.E., Madden, N.A., Dolan, L, & Wasik, B.A./ (1996) Success for All Thousand Oaks, CA: Corwin Press (ED397950).

Smith, L.D. Wood. W.R. (1996) B.F. Skinner and Behaviorism in American Culture Bethlehem, PA, Lehigh University Press 371-395

Socratic Method and Socratic Questions (6Types) retrieved October 20, 2005 from www.1000 advices.com/.../communicationquestions_socratic.html-Cached-Similar

Stahl, R (1994) The Essential Elements of Cooperative Learning in the Classroom Eric Digest retrieved December 4, 2005 www.ericdigest.org/1995/elements.httm

Tomlinson, C. (1995) Differentiate Instruction in Elementary Grades Eric Digest retrieved December 4, 2005 creep.crc.illinois.edu/archive/digest/2000/tomlinson.pdf

Ravitch, D. (2010) The Perspective of Diane Ravitch Exploring Educational Leadership, Vanguard School Administrators Association of New York Spring 2010.

Ravitch, D., (2010) Why I Changed My Mind About School Reform, The Wall Street Journal March 9, 2010 online.wsj.com/article/SB10001424052748704869304575109443305343 962.hrml. 16-21

Wagner, T. (2006) Rigor on Trial Education Week retrieved March 5, 2007 http://www.tonywagner.cpm/resources/rigor-on-trail

Wiggins, G., & McTighe, J. (1998) Understanding by Design Association for Supervision and Curriculum Department Alexandria Va Spring 2010 1-34

Wiggins, G., McTighe, J. (2007) Six Facets of Understanding by Design retrieved May 15 2008 http//www.huffenglish.com/?p=361-Cached-Similar

INDEX

V

Vanderbilt, Cornelius, 72
viewpoint and perspective, 80
Visual Arts SLC, 36, 65

W

Wagner, 58-59
walk-through, 74-75, 77, 81
walk-through form, 75
Ward, William Arthur, 50
Wiggins, Grant, 66
Wynn, Denise, 39

Edwards Brothers, Inc.
Thorofare, NJ USA
August 12, 2011